Adventures
of a
Migrant Heart
Finding Home in Every Place

By

Lina Bahlawan & Yemi Adefulu

ISBN

Hardcover: 978-1-967616-68-8

Paperback: 978-1-967616-56-5

Contents

Introduction

The journey of immigration is not for the faint of heart. It's a tough journey filled with challenges that push your strength and willpower to the limit. Yet, amidst the hardship and struggle, there also lies moments of awe-inspiring victories. For each migrant who embarks on this path, it is a journey that extends beyond mere physical boundaries and plunges deep into the core of our shared human experience.

The World Migration Report of 2024 reveals that one in every thirty individuals are migrants. This number only serves to highlight the immense courage and determination of those who choose to leave their homes and embark on a new life in a foreign land (World Migration Report, 2024).

In 2020, it was estimated that there were 281 million international migrants, representing approximately 3.6 per cent of the world's population. This number has been steadily rising over the last half-century, with a significant increase of 128 million from 1990 and almost triple the estimated number in 1970 (World Migration Report, 2024).

Despite the challenges and obstacles, each migrant's journey is unique and, ultimately, a triumph of the human spirit. It takes real courage to leave the familiar, start fresh in a new land, and build a life guided only by determination and hope. And for that, each migrant deserves our admiration and respect.

As immigrants ourselves, we—Lina Bahlawan and Yemi Adefulu—have traversed the intricate landscape that entails leaving familiar shores to chart a course on foreign soil.

We are deeply familiar with the profound emotional upheaval and practical challenges essential to the immigrant narrative. Our book is a product of our combined experiences and shared passion that aims to shed light on immigration's many facets through a vibrant mosaic of stories from fellow immigrants.

Before we delve deeper, allow us to introduce ourselves. My name is Lina Bahlawan, and I am constantly grappling with my identity due to my mixed heritage and upbringing spanning Jordan, Russia, and Canada. My childhood was shaped by the contrast between my Russian mother's traditional outlook and my Arabic father's progressive perspective. This cultural clash grew more complex when we moved to Canada, where the diversity exposed me to new customs and required significant adaptation.

Growing up in a multicultural household meant I was constantly exposed to different languages, customs, and traditions. It was both a blessing and a curse – while it enriched my understanding of the world and made me more open-minded, it also made me feel like an outsider at times. I often struggled with feeling like I didn't fully belong in any one culture.

This struggle only intensified when I moved to Canada at the age of seventeen. Suddenly, I found myself immersed in a completely different way of life – from the language to the food to the social norms. It was exciting and eye-opening but also brought a sense of loss for the familiar comforts of home.

As I grew older and built my own family, this feeling of displacement never truly went away. While I am proud of my diverse background and all that it has taught me, there are still moments where I long for a sense of belonging and yearn for a clear-cut identity. But through these experiences, I have learned that identity is not something fixed or definite – it is fluid and ever-evolving.

My name is Yemi Adefulu, and I am a global nomad—from living in Nigeria to the UK, to the Netherlands and Canada. I've been lucky to travel to 50 countries and get the chance to grapple with how to preserve my own heritage.

Growing up in Nigeria, I distinctly remember my father telling me a story about an extraordinary politician. He had the ability to effortlessly engage with diplomats from all over the world in one room and then seamlessly transition to deeply connecting with a group of local market women in the next. This story stayed with me as a child, sparking a desire to explore what unites us as humans instead of focusing on our differences. This desire to explore and understand different cultures led me to travel to various countries, where I found shared experiences and carried bits of each unique culture with me wherever I went.

My decision to attend university in Scotland transformed my life. I was welcomed into the close-knit Scottish community, captivated by the stunning landscapes, and enamored with the bold flavors of whiskey. The unique dialect, with its melodic cadences, may have been difficult for outsiders to understand, but it quickly became music to my ears. Scotland became my home, a place where I formed incredible bonds and cherished unforgettable experiences.

My next adventure led me to The Hague, where I intended to stay for two years. However, the charming Dutch architecture, serene dunes, and lively cycling culture won me over and captured my heart. A brief visit became eight years through which I embraced the lifestyle and had two lovely children.

Just as I felt settled in my Dutch life - living in a quaint 1950s home in Rijswijk - an opportunity arose to embark on a new adventure in a country very different from what I was used to: Canada.

My time in Canada has been eye-opening, with its diverse cuisine and the luxury of Vancouver's Westside. Here, I could ski in the mountains and then bask in the sun on the beach all in one day. Once again, I found myself surrounded by breathtaking natural beauty similar to Scotland, and even on the rainiest days, few cities can match the picturesque views of Vancouver.

Adapting to new societies has been a challenge and an opportunity that has helped me grow and see things differently. Reflecting on these experiences, I feel compelled to share them through this anthology of narratives—some my own, some fictional, and some from other immigrants—all aimed at focusing on the struggles and victories experienced by those who traverse similar paths.

Contained within these pages are diverse voices and experiences, each providing a unique lens into the immigrant journey. These narratives encapsulate the essence of starting afresh—the trials, triumphs, and enduring ties to one's roots that persist despite geographical distance.

We extend an invitation for you, our curious reader, to join us on this journey. As you immerse yourself in these stories, we hope they offer insight, foster empathy, inspire you, and deepen your comprehension.

Chapter One - What's in a name?

"A name is made for a child, and the child is made for a name."

- Sigmund Freud

The Power of a Name

Gently, I cradled the precious bundle in my arms, relishing the warmth of my newborn against my chest. His breaths were soft and faint, almost imperceptible, each one a reminder of the precious miracle of life. In the softly lit room, an air of admiration hung thickly as if reinforcing the sacred nature of this moment between father and child.

As I looked at the new life I had brought into the world, I was filled with wonder, love, and an unbreakable bond that would last forever.

"Adeyemi," I whispered, testing the traditional name on my tongue. I had always cherished this name, not just for its beautiful meaning - "I am worthy of the crown" - but also because it was a name both my father and I bore. It spoke of our rich heritage, our royal descent, and the values we held dear.

In the weeks before my son was born, I asked my father for his blessing to name him Adeyemi III. As I sat there, my mind raced, trying to find a way to honor our tradition while also embracing change for the future.

Beside me, Folake lay on the hospital bed, her exhaustion wrapped around her like a well-worn shawl. Yet her eyes danced with a joy that outshone the weariness etched into her features. She watched us, a smile curving her lips, and I felt the gravity of our shared journey.

"Perhaps we should consider an English name," she suggested, her voice a delicate thread in the quiet room. "Here, we must think of how he will walk through life and his name should open doors, not build walls."

"Are you saying our names are walls?" My voice was a murmur, a wave in the stillness.

She reached out, her hand finding mine. "No, love. But here, they are different. They sound... heavy to ears unaccustomed to the music of our homeland."

"Maybe," I whispered back, the uncertainty threading through my response. There was a tension between the past and the future, between where we came from and where we were now. Every moment, I was shaping my son's identity in a world very different from the one I knew.

"Whatever we choose," Folake murmured, reaching out to gently stroke the baby's cheek, "our son will know where he comes from, and he will also find his way wherever he goes."

"Of course," I said, my heart swelling with resolve. Our child would know the stories of Nigeria, the language, and the strength of our people. But he would also learn to navigate his way through the currents of this vast European society.

In that moment, I realized the true discussion point at hand: how to hold onto our roots while planting new ones. As immigrants, we were tasked with blending worlds and creating spaces where our children could thrive without forgetting the soil from which their families sprouted.

"Look at him, Adeyemi." Folake's voice pulled me back, her gaze fixed on the life we had created. "He's perfect."

"He is," I couldn't help but smile affectionately at the sight of her cradling our newborn son. As I bent down to give them both a gentle kiss on the forehead, my heart swelled with love and joy.

I sighed as my heart struggled with the choices, torn between the fear of being left out and the strong pride in our heritage. I needed to pick a name that honored both our past and the future we hoped for—a name as rich and beautiful as the new world we were adjusting to. A name that stood for not just identity but also hope.

We had to tread the line between two worlds to find the balance that would let him stand tall. I picked my son and held him closer, and somewhere in the quiet beating of his heart, I searched for an answer that would give him roots and wings.

The idea of naming him "Adeyemi III" seemed a fitting tribute, a continuation of our noble heritage. Still, I couldn't ignore the practical consideration of giving him an English name—something simpler and more familiar to those around us. This choice felt like a delicate balancing act between preserving our cultural roots and easing my child's path in a new world.

The dilemma of choosing a Moniker for a newborn is an enduring struggle faced by immigrants. The choices usually come down to picking a simpler, more English-sounding name to fit into the new culture easily or keeping a traditional name to stay connected to cultural roots. This decision is important, affecting both the child and the parents. A name is more than just a label; it has cultural, social, and personal meaning. Naming traditions around the world are based on long-held customs and meanings that reflect a society's values, beliefs, and history—showing one's heritage and identity.

Take African cultures as an example, where names are meticulously chosen to echo the unique circumstances surrounding a child's birth or to project aspirations for their future. Among Nigeria's Yoruba tribe, a popular name like Oluwatoyin—translating to "God is worthy of praise"—is more than just an identifier; it acts both as prayer and a daily reminder of faith. Similarly, in Igbo tradition names such as Chiamaka (God is beautiful) or Ifeanyi (Nothing is impossible with God) encapsulate spiritual and ethical values (Naming Traditions, 2023).

Asian cultures, too, attach significant importance to the symbolism behind names. In Japan, Sakura—a symbol of beauty and transience—is reminiscent of cherry blossoms' ephemeral bloom, showcasing the strong link between nature and aesthetics in Japanese naming conventions. In China, names like Li Wei can signify strength or prosperity (Blum, 1997).

Indian society often uses names that indicate caste affiliation, community ties, and religious beliefs. Surnames such as Sharma or Patel signal caste affiliations, while given names like Lakshmi (a Hindu goddess) reflect religious leanings (IndiNaming Customs, 2024).

Arab cultures carefully construct names that mirror lineage and social standing: Muhammad exudes praise, while Fatima bears profound cultural significance linked to Prophet Muhammad's daughter (Hawana, 1977).

Hispanic cultures cherish names deeply rooted in Catholicism. Using both paternal and maternal surnames honors both sides of the family. Names like Carlos symbolize a free spirit, while María reflects cultural identity and religious significance (Moore, 2017).

In Native American tribes, names are selected based on personal traits or significant life events. These names can evolve over time to reflect changing identities and experiences (Moore, 2017).

However, native English speakers often struggle with sounds from other languages that feel unfamiliar. When faced with names that are hard to pronounce, immigrants wonder: should I keep my name as it is or change it to make it easier for others to say?

One strategy might be to shorten the name into a form more digestible for English speakers. For example, "Ololade" could conveniently become "Lola," while "Giovanni" might morph into "John" Or "Gio." This process of simplification is prevalent among immigrants, with studies showing that many first-generation immigrants opt for a simplified version of their names to facilitate social integration (Carneiro & Reis, 2020).

Another route might involve picking an entirely new name that rolls off tongues easily in a different cultural setting. This could see "Xiaoyan," a Chinese scholar, adopting "Anna" as her alias during her stay abroad or someone named "Svetlana" choosing to respond to "Lana" (Carneiro & Reis, 2020).

In some instances, individuals may simply tweak their names' spelling or pronunciation to make them more appealing to others. For instance, "Xiao" could echo "Shawn," and "Anastasia" might truncate her journey by responding to "Ana" (Carneiro & Reis, 2020).

Some resolute individuals may choose to hold their ground, keeping their names intact despite inevitable mispronunciations. This decision can be a potent statement of cultural pride and identity.

In the end, the choices we make about names reflect a desire for connection and understanding in a world where many different names and cultures exist. Names link cultures together and help immigrants figure out their identities in new places. As societies become more multicultural, it's more important than ever to understand and respect the meaning of names. Naming isn't just about putting a label on something; it carries a person's heritage, values, and rich experiences in life. In making these decisions, immigrants navigate a complex journey of identity, culture, and belonging—one name at a time.

Determined Aspirations

Xiaojing's fingers danced across the keys with a rhythmic clack, each stroke a deliberate step toward her future. The glow of the computer screen illuminated her determined expression as she filled in the last fields of the application form. She was seated at her modest desk, which was cluttered with engineering textbooks, stacks of research papers on synthetic aviation fuel, and a mug of lukewarm green tea that had long been forgotten in the heat of the moment.

She paused, leaning back in her chair, and took a deep breath, letting the silence of the room wash over her. Xiaojing clicked on the tab labeled 'Experience,' her eyes scanning the bullet points that encapsulated years of dedication and hard work. Her qualifications were not just met but exceeded the job specifications for the manager position at the cutting-edge synthetic aviation fuel firm in Seattle.

A small, proud smile tugged at the corners of her lips as she read through her resume. She had ample years of experience and achievements that adorned her resume. Xiaojing's heart raced with the thought of leading a team of engineers to pilot this revolutionary technology. It wasn't just another job; it was a chance to help create a sustainable future and fulfill a dream that had started when she first got a chemistry set at seven.

"I will get it," she declared out loud to no one in particular, rather to herself, feeling the weight of the potential nestled in the pixels before her. This was more than an application; it represented her dreams, skills, and the determination that had driven her from one success to another.

"Mind if I take a look?" her husband asked, stepping into the room with the ease of familiarity.

"Of course," she replied, giving him space as he sat beside her to read through her resume, nodding approvingly at each bullet point detailing her accomplishments, her leadership qualities, and her vision. Then, pausing, he looked up from the page on the screen to meet her eyes, a question forming in his gaze. "Are you keeping your name?"

Xiaojing met his inquiry with an unflinching certainty. "Yeah"

Her name was a key part of her identity, representing every challenge she had overcome in her career. It carried the pride of her heritage, achievements, and unique perspective. To her, it wasn't just a sequence of letters—it was a declaration of who she was and what she had achieved.

He hesitated, the corners of his mouth twitching with a concern that danced in the furrow of his brow. "You know it's a tough name," he began, "They might think you're too foreign. I would recommend you use 'Jing' instead... it's easier for people to pronounce it."

Xiaojing felt the air stiffen between them, a carousel of emotions spinning silently in the space. Her name, etched into every diploma and commendation that adorned their walls, whispered of her roots and her journey. She leaned back in her chair, the leather creaking softly under the weight of her contemplation.

"Really?" She looked up at him, her voice steady but laden with a mixture of disbelief and disappointment. "You really think they would pass me by because of my name?"

"I really don't know, but do you want to take that chance?"

Navigating the vast expanse of today's global employment arena, the burden borne by a job seeker's name can substantially sway their odds of securing interview opportunities. Studies show that names with foreign or ethnic origins often lead to biases that harm career opportunities. This reflects personal prejudices and highlights deeper issues in hiring practices. The repercussions of such biases ripple beyond the immediate hurdles encountered by job hunters; they reverberate across entire sectors, shaping workplace ambiance and organizational efficacy.

A groundbreaking investigation spearheaded by economists scrutinized how names influence hiring results. The researchers dispatched fictitious resumes in response to job postings in Boston and Chicago, employing names that were either typically Caucasian—like Emily Walsh—or African American-sounding, such as Jamal Jones. The study unveiled a striking inconsistency: resumes with Caucasian monikers received 50% more callbacks than those bearing African American names. While the focus wasn't specifically on foreign names, these findings hint at a wider trend of discrimination based on perceived name ethnicity that likely impacts applicants with non-Western or ethnically diverse names. This occurrence is part of a broader matrix of unconscious biases that pervade recruitment processes, often unbeknownst to employers (Bertrand & Mullainathan, 2004).

To further frame this issue, consider statistics from the U.S. Equal Employment Opportunity Commission (EEOC), which revealed that minority groups continue to be underrepresented in numerous industries, particularly in higher-paying decision-making roles (EEOC, 2020).

For example, according to a 2020 report, Black, Hispanic, and Asian individuals collectively held merely 18.8% of managerial positions in Fortune 500 companies despite constituting a significantly larger portion of the workforce. The hurdles posed by name-based bias play an instrumental role in sustaining this underrepresentation, reinforcing pre-existing disparities and curtailing opportunities for diverse talent (Kurt, 2024).

Further corroborating this narrative is an exhaustive review by researchers proposed that biases stemming from names can dramatically curtail hiring odds for individuals from ethnic minority backgrounds. Their analysis offered proof that these biases often function subconsciously, swaying even well-meaning employers. Such dormant prejudices can fuel a cycle of underrepresentation across various sectors, particularly in leadership roles where diverse viewpoints are vital for innovation and problem-solving (Ziegert & Hanges, 2005).

For instance, a report by McKinsey & Company discovered that businesses in the top quartile for ethnic and racial diversity on executive teams were 36% more likely to outperform their industry counterparts in profitability. This association emphasizes the significance of diversity not merely as a societal benefit but as a crucial catalyst for business triumph (McKinsey & Company, 2020).

The reverberations of these biases extend far beyond individual job seekers—they pose serious concerns about diversity, equity, and inclusion within organizations. Companies oblivious to these biases and failing to implement proactive strategies risk bypassing valuable talent from diverse backgrounds, thus inhibiting innovation and growth. A 2019 study by the Boston Consulting Group found that diverse management teams generate 19% higher revenue due to innovation. This is especially pertinent in sectors that thrive on creativity and fresh ideas, like technology and marketing. By neglecting to harness the potential of a diverse workforce, organizations not only constrain their own success but also perpetuate systemic disparities (Forbes, 2021).

After the Wedding

At the wedding reception in Vancouver, I was drawn to Joe, a guest who radiated peace and wisdom from beyond this world. Our conversation turned to his heritage, the land, and the traditions full of timeless knowledge.

But then, Joe's serene expression turned serious as he gazed into the distance with a hint of sadness in his eyes. "You know," he said in a contemplative tone, "I've been struggling with my name."

Intrigued by his shift in demeanor, I leaned in closer. "What do you mean?"

After a moment of hesitation, Joe replied, "My name is not really Joe. It is Tuu-Tah-Qwees-Nup-Sheetl."

"Wow ... what does it mean?" I asked, curious.

"Which means 'Responsibility of the Teaching of the Land," he smiled with pride.

"Then why do you go by Joe?" I prodded further, intrigued by the internal conflict I could feel in Joe, or rather Tuu-Tah-Qwees-Nup-Sheetl.

With a heavy sigh, Joe explained, "As a child, I was sent to a residential school. We were forced to adopt English names and abandon our true identities. In that system, I became Joe - a name that assimilated me into their world."

I could see the turmoil etched on his face. "So, Tuu-Tah-Qwees-Nup-Sheetl holds a much deeper significance for you?"

"Yes," Joe replied with a heavy nod. "It's more than just a name; it represents my role in the community and my duty to pass down the wisdom of the land. Lately, I've come to this realization - how can I truly share our traditions and teachings if I'm not fully embracing the name that embodies them?"

His words weighed heavily on him. "It feels like I'm trying to convey my heritage while keeping a part of it hidden." I couldn't help but feel deep empathy for him.

"Reclaiming your native name seems like a way to honor and integrate your heritage into your life completely." I thought out loudly.

Joe's expression softened with relief. "Yes, exactly. Embracing Tuu-Tah-Qwees-Nup-Sheetl goes beyond just using my birth name; it's about staying true to the teachings of the land and fulfilling my role in the community. It's a way to bridge my past and present."

As we talked, I couldn't stop thinking about Joe's deep realization. His struggle showed that even locals aren't immune to the challenges immigrants face over something as simple as their name.

The celebration carried on, but Joe's epiphany left a lasting impact, weaving a thread of conflicted emotions into the fabric of the evening.

Chapter Two- Language Part I: Voices Across Language Borders

"Language shapes the way we think and determines what we can think about."

– Benjamin Lee Whorf

Cultural Threads

Sitting on the edge of my mother's bed, I studied the complicated patterns of her quilt. Our home was a tapestry of cultures and languages, with my Arabic father and Russian mother. Growing up in Amman, Jordan I was fluent in both tongues, but today, I was struggling to find the right words to express the hurt I had been feeling for a while now. My heart weighed heavy with a child's confusion, silenced by the walls my father built around himself.

"Mama," I whispered, the word a breath of warm air in the cool room. "Why doesn't Baba call me his ray of sunshine? Like you do."

My mother set aside her knitting, the click-clack of needles pausing mid-stitch. Her eyes, deep pools reflecting years spent beneath the vast Russian skies, sought mine with an understanding that seemed to stretch beyond the years I had lived.

"Ah, Lina," she began, her voice a gentle chime amidst the quiet, "In Russia," she explained gently, "Sunshine is rare and coveted. It warms our bones and lifts our spirits through the long winters." She reached out, her hand brushing a lock of hair from my forehead, a touch as light as the kiss of the sun itself. "But here, in Jordan, the sun is a fiery giant in the sky, a relentless presence... So, your Baba shows his love in other ways."

"In what ways?" I frowned, my eyebrows drawing together in protest, believing wholeheartedly that my father's lack of endearment terms for me meant one thing: his lack of love for me.

My heart raced as this thought hit me, growing in intensity far beyond my naive years.

"Your Baba," Mama smiled softly. "He has his own way of showing love." She paused. "He calls you 'like a cool breeze?'"

I had heard the word before, slipping out amidst the fluid cadence of Arabic during our evening talks on the terrace. Breeze. I had always thought it was just another word, a nickname without weight.

"It's not just a word," she continued, sensing my confusion. "In this desert land, a breeze is a life—it cools, it soothes, it brings relief from the relentless sun."

The chair scraped the floor as I leaned in. Could this language of love that had always eluded me really be so simple, so basic?

"So, he does love me... just differently?" I stutter the words, still unsure if I truly understand

"More than you know, моя солнце," she replied, using the Russian term with a tender smile. "And you are his sunshine too, just in ways you're learning to see."

I nodded, a seed of comprehension planting itself within me. Love can be expressed differently in different languages.

Language, as we know it, is the primary tool of human interaction. It is a collection of words arranged in specific and accepted patterns expressed through speech, writing, or gestures. This communication system is unique to particular nations or groups, embodying cultural nuances and social practices. While this definition captures the structural aspects of language, it misses the emotional connection we share with it. Our thoughts are closely tied to our native language and translating them into another language isn't just about finding the right words. It's about changing the meanings to fit the new language. This makes us wonder how language affects the way we see things, shapes our thoughts, and even influences our reality.

The Sapir-Whorf hypothesis provides a compelling framework for understanding these relationships. It posits that the structure of a language affects its speakers' worldview and cognition. One well-known illustration of this concept is the "Russian Blues" phenomenon. In Russian, there are two distinct words for blue: 'goluboy' refers to light blue, while 'siniy' denotes dark blue. In contrast, English employs a single term to encompass both shades. Research indicates that Russian speakers can differentiate between light and dark blue more quickly than their English-speaking counterparts. This distinction suggests that the linguistic categorization of color influences perception and cognitive processing (Green, 2023).

A pivotal study explored this notion further, demonstrating that Russian speakers were more adept at distinguishing between light and dark blue hues when presented with them on a color continuum. The researchers used a series of color swatches that varied subtly from light to dark blue and found that Russian participants could identify the colors more rapidly than English speakers. This study supports the idea that linguistic categories can shape our cognitive processes, ultimately affecting how we perceive the world around us (Winawer, Witthoft., Frank, Wu, & Boroditsky, 2007).

Building on this premise, researchers from the Norwegian University of Science and Technology (NTNU) and the University of Oslo investigated how bilingualism affects color perception, focusing on Lithuanian and Norwegian speakers' identification of various shades. Like Russian, Lithuanian has separate terms for blue: 'žydra' for light blue and 'mėlyna' for dark blue, whereas Norwegian uses the singular term 'blå.' Their study showed that bilingual participants' ability to tell colors apart was influenced by the language they used. When they spoke Lithuanian, they were more accurate in distinguishing shades, suggesting that language activates mental frameworks that help with perception.

Dr. Mila Vulchanova, a researcher involved in the study, emphasized that these results illuminate the intricate relationship between language and sensory perception. Our brains respond more readily to the activated language that links sensory experiences with linguistic context. This connection suggests that language does not merely serve as a medium for communication; it also shapes how we interpret and engage with our environment (Haugan, 2024).

The impact of language goes beyond color perception. Research in cognitive linguistics shows that language shapes how we understand time, space, and emotions. For example, studies have shown that speakers of languages with different ways of describing space navigate their surroundings in unique ways.

English speakers and speakers of the Guugu Yimithirr language (Indigenous Australian language spoken in the Far North Queensland region), which uses cardinal directions instead of egocentric directions, approached navigation tasks differently. While English speakers relied on personal orientation (left and right), Guugu Yimithirr speakers used geographical directions (north and south), showcasing how language shapes cognitive strategies (Kiang, 2019).

Furthermore, the language we use can influence our emotional experiences. Research highlights how bilingual individuals often report different emotional responses when using their second language compared to their native tongue. This difference can be attributed to varying degrees of emotional resonance and cultural context tied to each language. For example, an English speaker might talk about love or loss in Spanish in a way that feels more distant, as the emotions may not fully come through in the translation. This shows how language is closely connected to our emotions, affecting not just how we communicate but also how we feel and relate to the world (Pavlenko, 2005).

In conclusion, language is far more than a mere collection of words or a tool for communication; it is a complex system that shapes our thoughts, influences our perceptions, and informs our emotional experiences. Through the lens of the Sapir-Whorf hypothesis and the myriad studies examining language's impact on cognition, we gain insight into the profound connections between language and human experience. By acknowledging the intricate relationship between language and perception, we can better appreciate the richness of human communication and the diverse ways in which we navigate and understand our world.

Counting in French

My fingers danced over the keyboard, typing out translations from English to French like a pianist nailing a tricky piece. Growing up multilingual has always kept me grounded in the whirlwind of different cultures. From the twists of Russian Cyrillic to the curves of Arabic, every language opened up a new world for me. But now, here in the charming cobblestone streets of Montreal, Canada, French feels like the key to fitting in and finding work.

In a cozy corner of a busy café, with the smell of fresh coffee and croissants in the air, I started to explore this new language. The city's energy matched the lively French language, blending old charm with modern energy. As I practiced verbs and phrases, I felt the rhythm of the language match my heartbeat, creating a flow of mind and instinct.

I couldn't believe all the cool stuff I was learning, like little treasures hidden in the language. It wasn't just about memorizing words or getting the accent right; it was about understanding the culture behind them. Every time I made a sentence, I could feel the nuances and layers of meaning that make up French communication. These little wins boosted my self-esteem and gave me hope that I could express myself in even more places around the globe.

I read the next phrase, "Tu me manques," and it struck a familiar chord within me, but with a twist. Like wearing a sweater backward, it was a different way of expressing missing someone. Instead of saying "I miss you," it puts the focus on the person being missed. I pondered this new perspective and savored the uniqueness of the phrase, letting it linger in the café like an unfinished song.

As I turned the page, I was faced with the French numbers jumping and dancing around like an arithmetic ballet. Seventeen wasn't just seventeen. It was "ten and seven" - "dix-sept" in French. And eighteen followed suit, known as "ten and eight" or "dix-huit." Each number felt like a little math problem that I had to pause and solve.

As I sat in the quaint café, sipping on a steaming cup of coffee, my mind was captivated by the curious case of eighty – "quatre-vingts" – literally four twenties. I raised an eyebrow, my mind playfully juggling the numbers and marveling at their historical significance. It was a testament to the language's complex layers, a numeric relic that held its ground in modern speech.

With a pencil in hand, I wrote down the number and traced its digits like they were clues to an ancient puzzle. Surrounded by the noise of the café and the sound of my pencil, I became deeply fascinated by the unique details of my new language learning.

Images of Blaise Pascal and his primitive calculator, the Pascaline, flashed through my mind. Perhaps he, too, had chuckled at the same numeric oddity that now intrigued me. Or maybe Joseph Fourier's groundbreaking work on heat flow was sparked by this very same source of numeric novelty that gave "soixante-dix" and "quatre-vingts" more depth than just mere numbers.

As I took another sip of my coffee, the clink of cups and murmur of patrons around me faded into a quiet hum. My thoughts swirled with *possibilities as I delved deeper into the connection between language and mathematics. Here I was, a student of languages unexpectedly brushing against the hem of mathematical history through the quirks of French numerals. It felt like a beautiful tapestry woven with threads of language and logic, revealing intricate patterns that connected words to numbers and ideas to eras.*

Lost in contemplation, I felt a newfound respect for the puzzle of French I was resolute to solve—a language that not only shaped speech but also influenced how we perceive and understand the world around us.

Language, much like a master sculptor, expertly carves the manner in which its users engage in dialogue. It doesn't just govern what is expressed but also the method of expression, infusing exchanges with distinct shades and textures. The complexities of language impact not only word choice but also the foundational cultural values and societal norms that direct communication. Languages can either talk around a topic, rely a lot on context, or go straight to the point with clear precision. This difference reflects the variety of communication styles found in different cultures.

Consider Japanese as an example. Its conversations often encapsulate indirectness and sensitivity to context, akin to an elegant ballet of honorifics and nuanced expressions. This linguistic design reflects Japan's profound regard for politeness and social harmony. In Japanese culture, upholding harmony and steering clear of confrontation are crucial. A Japanese speaker is unlikely to make a blunt request or assertion. Instead, they skillfully use euphemisms and hints to steer through potentially awkward situations.

For instance, if a Japanese person wishes to exit an event, they might subtly signal their intent by remarking, "It's getting late, isn't it?" This roundabout approach allows the listener to deduce the speaker's intention without any direct confrontation in social settings, as it helps maintain harmony and respect.

Furthermore, the formality level of the language changes based on the relationship between speakers. Japanese uses different degrees of politeness via honorifics and verb forms that indicate social status and relationship dynamics. For instance, someone younger speaking to an elder would opt for more formal language, underlining their respect for seniority. This sophisticated form of communication underscores cultural emphasis on hierarchy and social relationships (Nishimura, Nevgi & Tella, 2008).

In sharp contrast are languages such as German, Russian, and Dutch, which resemble straight highways rather than meandering paths in terms of communication. These languages are structured to facilitate clear expression and lucidity. For example, German communication highlights directness. German values addressing matters without unnecessary frills. In professional scenarios where time is crucial, a German speaker might plainly state, "The report is overdue; we need it by the end of the day."

Germans appreciate direct communication in workplace settings, linking it with efficiency and productivity. This straightforwardness extends to personal interactions as well, where clarity often trumps ambiguity.

Similarly, Russian communication tends to be direct rather than diplomatic. A Russian speaker might just say, "You need to finish this task," focusing on clarity and urgency. Studies show that Russians believe direct communication helps with better understanding at work. While Russians can use different levels of formality for important information or feedback, clarity is usually the most important (Livermore, 2013).

Dutch speakers also prioritize frankness. Renowned for their efficiency and practicality, Dutch communication generally avoids complex language. A Dutch individual might tersely say, "This approach isn't working; let's try something else," focusing on the effectiveness and clarity of the message rather than skirting around feelings.

In North America, communication styles represent a balanced mix of directness and diplomacy molded by cultural norms that emphasize both individualism and efficiency. In the United States and Canada, people generally appreciate straightforward communication while also incorporating elements of politeness and tactfulness. For instance, an American might say, "I think we need to reconsider our strategy." This statement is clear yet softened by its framing as a suggestion rather than an order.

Americans believe politeness is important in professional communication, highlighting a cultural tendency towards balancing assertiveness with respect. Canadians, known for their polite demeanor, often use indirect language to avoid confrontation while still effectively conveying their points. Instead of bluntly disagreeing with someone's idea, Canadians might express their dissent by saying, "I'm not sure if this is the best approach." This gentle expression of disagreement maintains respect throughout the conversation, aligning with the Canadian cultural value of politeness (Lingua Link DC, 2022).

These different communication styles show how language and culture work together to shape unique ways of interacting. Japanese communication is shaped by a culture that values politeness, which leads to indirect speech and hidden meanings. On the other hand, German, Russian, and Dutch languages mix directness with clarity and practicality, focusing on clear and efficient communication.

By acknowledging the nuances of language and its connection to culture, we can foster more effective and respectful interactions. Language serves as a powerful tool for connection and understanding its artistry allows us to engage with others more meaningfully. As we navigate the complexities of global communication, let us embrace the richness of linguistic diversity, appreciating the artistry that shapes our interactions.

New Beginnings in The Hague

As I emerged from the taxi, my eyes were drawn to the towering building that would soon become my new workplace in The Hague - the capital city of South Holland in the Netherlands. It had been just two weeks since my family and I made the move from the UK for this incredible opportunity.

My heart raced with nervous excitement as I went through security. This was my chance to start over and create a new life in a place I didn't know.

The office was impressive. It was modern and shiny, with lots of glass and chrome. As I walked down the hall, I looked at my reflection in one of the windows. I wore a smart outfit - an oxford shirt, sweater vest, and tailored pants - hoping to make a good first impression.

I arrived at the conference room ten minutes early, eager to meet my new colleagues. As I entered, they were already gathered around the large table.

The meeting began promptly, and introductions were made. When it was my turn to speak, all eyes turned to me. Trying my best to hide my overexcitement, I stood up straight and confidently addressed the group.

"Hello, everyone," I began with a warm smile. "My name is Yemi. I am thrilled to be joining this team and can't wait to dive into the exciting projects we have ahead."

With a brief yet friendly summary of my background, I was welcomed into the meeting by Emma's nod. As I observed the dynamics around me, the exchanges were brisk and precise, almost surgical in their delivery. Unlike the often-circuitous dialogue back home, there was something uplifting but intimidating about this directness.

Jeroen sat at the head of the table, his features sharp and unreadable. With an air of authority, he leaned forward, commanding attention without demanding it. "Emma," his voice rang out with crisp clarity, "the report you submitted—it won't fly with the client."

The room went quiet, and everyone watched as Jeroen and Emma had a tense conversation. I noticed Jeroen's steady gaze and calm posture, with his hands flat on the table. It was clear he had power and respect among his coworkers.

"It's lacking two key elements," Jeroen continued his words cutting through the stillness of the room. "The risk assessment and market analysis that I outlined in my last email."

Emma's posture remained relaxed yet attentive as she nodded slowly, processing each word deliberately. A strand of hair fell across her forehead, but she didn't seem bothered by it as she maintained her unwavering focus on Jeroen. The weight of expectation hung palpably in the room as they continued their discussion.

Emma's reply was poised and composed, her tone betraying no hint of irritation or surprise. "I will incorporate those points into the revised version and have it delivered to you by the week's end," she stated confidently, scribbling a few notes on her pad with a swift and decisive stroke of her pen.

As I thought about my own reactions to such directness, my mind turned inward. Back in London, office politics were full of passive-aggressive comments and hidden hints. Could I adjust to this new way? Would I be able to handle criticism as directly as Jeroen's?

I pictured myself in Emma's shoes, receiving pointed feedback in front of new colleagues. There would undoubtedly be a sting, a momentary surge of defensiveness. But beneath that initial reaction, I couldn't help but feel a budding admiration for the clarity and efficiency it brought. No need for second-guessing or wasted time.

"Thank you, Emma," Jeroen interjected, snapping me out of my reverie. "Let's move on."

The meeting carried on, and I listened intently as everyone gave their updates, making mental notes of each person and their respective work responsibilities.

As the meeting came to an end, I stood up, and Emma approached me with a warm smile. "Welcome aboard," she greeted warmly.

"Thank you," I said, my voice hesitant as I asked, "Are you okay?" Her eyes widened with confusion at my question.

"Yes...why do you ask?" she replied, her expression searching.

"Well, Jeroen seemed a bit too direct, don't you think?" A warm smile spread across my face.

"Oh," she chuckled, understanding my concern. "We're Dutch...this is just how we communicate."

I felt a sense of relief wash over me as I realized it was simply a cultural difference.

As I walked out of the meeting room, I couldn't help but feel excited for what the future held. The possibilities were endless, and I was eager to make meaningful contributions to this dynamic team.

Chapter Three - Language Part II: The edge of multilingual skills

"To have another language is to possess a second soul."

– Charlemagne

Heritage through Language

Arjun slumped over his textbook, the Sanskrit letters swimming before his eyes like an indecipherable code. He dragged his pencil along the margins of his notebook, etching doodles that mirrored the frustration knotting his brows. The intricate characters, each a labyrinth of curves and lines, seemed to mock him from the page. Why should he care about words that felt so aloof from the skyscrapers and bustling streets of Toronto?

"Thamasi ma jyotir gamaya," he mumbled, the ancient plea for enlightenment feeling ironic on his tongue. He couldn't see the light, not here, not in these symbols that seemed as relevant to his life as the mythical chariots they described. He was supposed to translate the sentence, but the task felt as intimidating as crossing oceans without a compass.

The room around him buzzed with the usual sounds of their home in Canada—cars honking outside, neighbors talking as they walked their dogs, and sometimes a siren blaring through the air. This was his world, where Hindi didn't matter, where people spoke English or French, and where his classmates would probably laugh if he spoke his parents' language.

"Why do I need this?" he whispered into the quiet room, half hoping the walls would answer back with a reason. Gaya, the city of his parents' stories, was a mere whisper of tales and traditions, a place held together by the threads of nostalgia rather than the concrete reality of his life in Toronto. Arjun knew more about hockey scores and maple leaves than

about cricket or the prayers and festivals that had shaped his family's past.

He sighed and pushed the textbook away, feeling both stubborn and tired. To him, it was just homework—useless exercises in a language that didn't fill the streets of his city, with its tall glass and steel buildings. He wanted to ignore it, but deep down, he knew the words were more than just symbols on a page. They were a part of his family's history, even if he was too young to fully understand what that meant.

Neha's silhouette appeared in the doorway, her sari a cascade of vibrant colors against the muted walls of their Toronto home.

"Arjun," she called out gently, a smile playing on her lips as she adjusted the small diya lamp on the bookshelf. The flickering light caught the gold threads in her attire, making them dance like the sun on the Ganges River at dawn.

"Kaise ho, beta?" Neha's voice was like a gentle caress as she bent down to peek at his work, her hands still carrying the fragrant scent of marigolds from the garlands she had been stringing together for the festivities. Arjun glanced up from his papers, the characters on them blurring in front of his tired eyes. He couldn't help but feel a sense of comfort and warmth radiating from his mother.

"Fine, Mom," he muttered half-heartedly, his troubled expression belying his words.

Neha straightened up, her gaze sweeping across their living space that was slowly being transformed in anticipation of Diwali. The room seemed to come alive with the vibrant colors and scents of the festival. She moved with purpose. As she hummed an old Hindi lullaby, its sweet melody floated through the air, mingling with the hypnotic aroma of incense.

"Are you excited about Diwali?" Neha asked with a smile. Her eyes sparkled with joy and anticipation as she continued to prepare for the celebration.

Arjun's face finally lit up with a small smile of his own as he replied, "Yeah...I can't wait for all the delicious sweets."

"Diwali is much more than just lights and sweets, Arjun," she explained, pausing to light another diya and place it carefully on the windowsill. "It's the victory of good over evil, of light over darkness." As she spoke, the shadows in the room seemed to retreat, conceding to the soft glow that now enveloped them both. "We clean our homes, prepare delicious food, and gather with loved ones to remember that, no matter how dark it gets, there will always be a spark to guide us through."

Outside, the Toronto skyline stood tall, untouched by stories of gods, demons, and ancient battles. But inside their small apartment, the tale of Rama returning to Ayodhya after defeating Ravana was coming alive, one diya at a time. Diwali, the festival of lights, was Neha's way of holding onto her heritage—a heritage she hoped to share with her son, even though it felt so far from their life in Canada.

"Each light is a reminder," she continued, her voice soft but resolute. "That knowledge, hope, and compassion are the true treasures we should seek and share. It connects us, Arjun, to something timeless—to our history, our values, and to each other."

Though the significance of her words may have eluded Arjun, the atmosphere of admiration and beauty did not.

"Mom," he muttered, almost hoping she wouldn't hear, "Can I just stop when I'm 10?"

Neha paused, her hands still holding a string of marigolds intended for the living room archway. She turned, her gaze settling upon her son with a mixture of understanding and firm resolve.

"Arjun," she began, kneeling beside him, "This language is the melody of our ancestors. It's more than words and sentences; it's the rhythm of our heritage."

She reached out, gently correcting the hold of his pencil. "Learning connects you to where you come from, to the stories and wisdom passed down through generations. It's a gift, my dear, and one day, I hope you'll see the beauty in its embrace, just as we see the beauty in the lights of Diwali."

The journey of preserving one's native tongue amidst the bustling cosmopolitanism of a new country is a complex dance of cultural ties, family traditions, societal influences, and personal drives. As immigrants find their footing in unfamiliar territories, the struggle to keep their mother languages alive becomes not just a quest for self-identity but also an endeavor to safeguard their cultural legacy.

Language is more than just grammar and vocabulary. It serves as a live reminder of a people's history, culture, and legacy. Children who are skilled in their original languages have a greater understanding of their cultural roots. Their sense of belonging and self-worth are increased by this connection to their heritage, highlighting the significance of language preservation for immigrant families (Alshihry, 2024).

Consider this: the majority of first-generation immigrants prioritize passing on their mother tongue to their children (Statics Canada, 2016). This stems from the conviction that maintaining linguistic ties will gift them with an enriched sense of identity and deeper insight into their heritage. Moreover, shared language can strengthen familial bonds as it fosters improved communication and understanding within families.

Family dynamics play a crucial role in preserving the language. Parents often don the hat of primary language teachers. Families who actively converse in their native languages at home are more likely to pass it down to future generations successfully. A study published in The International Journal found higher levels of fluency among children from families that allocate specific times for speaking in their mother tongues (Thomas & Collier, 2001).

A lot of families use tactics like "language nights" or attend cultural gatherings where they speak their native tongues. For example, Indian families may actively use Hindi during Diwali celebrations, which would reinforce both language proficiency and cultural values at the same time.

However, societal pressures can pose formidable challenges to language preservation efforts. Dominant cultures often prioritize proficiency in mainstream languages, leading to a "language shift." A report reveals that majority of immigrant parents worry their children might prioritize English over their mother tongues due to societal influences. This shift is particularly noticeable in educational environments where English is the medium of instruction, further complicating the challenge (Poole, 2019).

Wanting to fit in can make parents focus on their children learning the main language, sometimes ignoring their own native language. Immigrant parents think speaking English well is important for school success. Because of this, their native language may become less important over time.

Generational differences significantly impact language preservation. First-generation immigrants are typically more proficient in their native languages, while subsequent generations may become less fluent. "Hasson's (2006) study of Miami-area Latino students showed that although 90.6% claimed Spanish as their first language, 75.2% were English dominant, and only 24.3% felt equally comfortable in Spanish and English" (Poole, 2019).

Despite these challenges, many immigrant families successfully employ methods to promote language preservation - formal education, community engagement, and technology utilization being key among them.

Formal education plays a pivotal role in preserving languages. Many families opt for bilingual education programs that foster the learning of both the native and dominant languages concurrently. Institute for Immigration, Globalization, and Education indicates students enrolled in bilingual programs perform better academically and demonstrate higher proficiency levels in their mother tongues.

Dual-language immersion programs have gained popularity in recent years. A study by the Center for Research on Education, Diversity & Excellence found students enrolled in such programs scored 20% higher in reading proficiency compared to monolingual peers (Thomas & Collier, 2001).

Language preservation also benefits from community involvement. Language instruction and cultural events are frequently offered by immigrant communities' cultural centers and organizations. Hispanic groups, for example, usually host festivals honoring their culture that heavily emphasize Spanish (Lopez, Krogstad & Flores, 2018).

In the digital era, technology plays a crucial role in language preservation. Language-learning apps and online resources are increasingly used to supplement children's learning. Apps such as Duolingo or Rosetta Stone can provide an engaging platform for children to practice their mother tongues, making language preservation more accessible. Social media platforms also offer opportunities for families to connect with others who speak their native languages, fostering a sense of community and shared experience.

Two specific cases are worth sharing; these cases provide a compelling example of successful language retention in the Indian American Community and The Hispanic American Community

Many Indian families actively engage in cultural practices that reinforce their native languages, such as celebrating festivals like

Diwali and participating in community events organized by local temples. Many Indian immigrants speak their native language at home, including Hindi, Telugu, Gujarati, Tamil, and Punjabi, according to the migration policy institute, more than 66% of Indians immigrants speak their native language at home (Greene & Batalova, 2024).

Similarly, Many Hispanic families encourage their children to speak Spanish at home while also participating in cultural events that celebrate their heritage. According to the Pew Research Center, 88% of Hispanic adults in the U.S. believe it is very important for future generations to speak Spanish, reflecting a strong commitment to cultural preservation (Lopez, Krogstad & Flores, 2018).

For immigrants, maintaining their native tongue involves a dance with many partners, including generational differences, social expectations, and family ties. Despite all of these obstacles, many immigrant families manage to preserve their mother tongues, acting as guardians of their cultural identities and heritage for future generations.

As our society morphs into a vibrant mosaic of cultures, the role of language retention takes on a new significance. It's not merely an act that enriches personal identities but also one that adds colorful threads to the wider community's cultural fabric. By standing behind these immigrant families in their endeavor to preserve their languages, we are nurturing a society that doesn't just tolerate diversity but revels in it. The quest for language retention isn't just about keeping words from fading; it's about protecting identities, histories, and the rich heritage that gives our world its unique contour.

Family Visit

The hum of the aircraft's engines provided a constant backdrop as I glanced at Tamara and Rula, their faces pressed against the small oval windows. Their eyes danced with reflections of clouds, painted in hues of sunset oranges and twilight purples as we sailed above the Atlantic, closing the distance between Montreal and Alexandria.

"Mom," Tamara whispered, her voice barely audible above the steady thrum of the aircraft. "What if we can't talk to them?"

Rula turned her head, nodding in silent agreement with her sister's worry.

I squeezed Tamara's hand comfortingly and brushed a lock of hair away from Rula's face. "You know, most people there will speak some English," I said, infusing my voice with as much confidence as I could muster. "And everyone will be so happy to see you that it won't matter much."

"Really?" Tamara asked, her eyes searching mine for certainty.

"Really," I affirmed, smiling. "Plus, between hugs and smiles, who needs too many words?"

They both offered me tentative smiles. The idea of language, an invisible wall between them and their family, loomed in their young minds.

"Besides," I continued, "You two are experts at charades. Remember when you acted out the entire plot of 'The Lion King' for me?"

A giggle escaped Tamara, and Rula's shoulders relaxed slightly. "Yeah, that was fun," she conceded.

"Exactly," I said. "And if all else fails, we'll have a crash course in Arabic using hands and feet." I wiggled my fingers and toes, eliciting a laugh from them both.

"Okay," Tamara sighed, her anxiety ebbing away like the tide. "We'll manage."

The reality of our arrival dawned as the plane taxied along the runway after landing with a soft thump. The welcoming embrace of the

Mediterranean air embraced us as we unloaded and navigated the busy airport.

"Mom, look!" Tamara tugged at my sleeve, pointing toward the group of people gathered just beyond customs.

There they were: aunts with open arms, uncles with broad smiles, and cousins jumping up and down, all of them chatting away in rapid Arabic. My heart swelled at the sight, a tapestry of familiar faces and sounds enveloping us as we stepped forward into their midst.

"Ahlan wa sahlan!" their voices rang out in unison, the traditional greeting washing over us like a wave.

"Marhaba," I replied, my own Arabic rusty, as Tamara and Rula shyly echoed the word. The family surged forward, laughter mingling with greetings as hands reached out to pull us into a flurry of embraces. Each kiss planted on our cheeks was a punctuation mark in the story of our reunion, a story written in a language my children heard but did not speak.

Yet, amidst the sea of foreign syllables, I saw Tamara and Rula's eyes widen with wonder, their initial hesitation melting away under the warmth of familial love. At that moment, I knew that no barrier of language could diminish the connection that bound us all together.

It wasn't long before we found ourselves on the sandy shores of a bustling beach, the Mediterranean lapping at our feet. The family had congregated around a cluster of worn wooden tables. A feast spread out before us. Platters of grilled fish, garnished with slices of lemon, garlic, and olive oil, commanded the center stage, surrounded by a chorus of Tahini sauce, Hummus, and pita bread. I watched as Tamara and Rula hesitated, then reached out to fill their plates, their movements tentative but curious.

"Fish is good?" Uncle Youssef asked Rula in halting English, pointing to the plate before him. Rula nodded enthusiastically, her mouth full, her expression one of blissful approval. "Yes, very!" she managed between bites.

"Sun is nice, yes?" Auntie Hala smiled at Tamara, her hands making a gesture that encompassed the golden light and the gentle breeze. Tamara's smile was wide as she responded, "Yes, it's beautiful here."

It was a dance of simple words and shared experiences, a bridge constructed over the gap of language. Questions about the school, favorite colors, and the coldness of Canadian winters were exchanged, broken English mingling with laughter and the occasional helping hand of translation from a bilingual cousin or me.

The children from the extended family darted around us, their games a swirl of motion and Arabic exclamations. Tamara and Rula watched, a flicker of longing in their eyes to join in, yet they remained on the periphery, sipping their sodas and nibbling on the flaky flesh of their fish.

"Later," I whispered to them, catching their gaze, "You'll see how easy it will be to connect without needing many words." They nodded, still unsure but bolstered by the friendly exchanges thus far, the universal language of kindness speaking louder than any words could.

The moon hung low, a silver crescent in the balmy Egyptian night. I was leaning against the balcony railing of my aunt's house, watching the palm trees sway gently in the sea breeze, when Tamara emerged from the shadows, her small figure illuminated by the kitchen light spilling out through the open door.

"Hey," she said softly, her voice barely rising above the distant sounds of laughter and the lapping waves.

"Hey, sweetie." I turned to her, noticing the way her eyes lingered on the children playing a raucous game of tag in the courtyard below.

She leaned on the railing beside me, her brows knitting together slightly. "Mom, I wish you had taught us Arabic," she murmured, her gaze fixed on the scene below.

I tilted my head, inviting her to elaborate, though I already sensed the weight of her thoughts.

"Today, during the games, I felt...out of place." She hesitated before continuing. "It was like they had to hit pause every time they tried to include me. They were super nice about it, but I could tell it was awkward for them to stop and explain everything in English."

I frowned, feeling a twinge of guilt. "I know it's not easy... I should've considered teaching you both the language. It's part of who you are, part of our heritage... but between learning French and English, I thought adding Arabic might be too much."

She sighed, resting her chin on her hands. "I just wanted to be part of it all, you know? Not the one slowing things down or causing trouble because I can't understand."

"Language is a bridge, true," I admitted, "But it's not the only way to connect. You're still part of this family, and they love you—language barrier and all."

Tamara looked up at me, her eyes searching for reassurance. "Do you think we could learn some words while we're here? Just so I can play with them without needing someone to translate?"

"Of course, we can try," I promised, wrapping an arm around her shoulders. "And when we get back home, if you're willing, we'll find a way to keep learning. Okay?"

"Okay." A small smile tugged at her lips, and she relaxed into the embrace. "Thanks, Mom."

"Anything for you, kiddo." I squeezed her shoulder, watching as she cast another longing glance at the lively game below. Tomorrow would be another day and, perhaps, with a few new words, a fresh start.

Chapter Four- Language Part III: A World of Accents

"Language is a living entity, and accents are its many faces."

— Anonymous

Where are you from?

Emeka stood before the crowd, a mosaic of faces reflecting the diversity that mirrored his own journey. His hands, once calloused from the red earth of Nigeria, now gestured with a refined elegance that had come from years of adaptation and survival in foreign lands.

"Thank you all for coming," he began, his voice carrying a subtle musicality that seemed to dance between continents. It was a blend of sounds, like an auditory tapestry woven through time and experience, each thread representing a different chapter of his life.

The 'r's rolled off his tongue with a Scottish burr he'd picked up in Edinburgh, where the cold, gray sky often matched the granite underfoot. Then, a lively Australian twang laced his speech, a souvenir from sunsoaked days down under, where he'd learned to replace "hello" with "g'day" and toss "mate" into casual conversation as easily as a boomerang.

And now here he was, in Canada, where his accent had softened yet again like the autumnal leaves of the vast Canadian woodlands. It was a curious mix that prompted one to listen not just to the words spoken but also to the story they told—a story of movement, change, and resilience.

As Emeka spoke, his voice changed in small ways, just like his life had—always adapting and changing but always connected to his Nigerian roots. The audience was captivated not only by his knowledge but also by the way he spoke, which made him stand out as someone with a global perspective—a man whose voice connected people from different cultures and backgrounds.

Emeka adjusted his glasses as he surveyed the room, a sea of expectant faces reflecting the soft glow of the projector. The clicker in his hand felt like an extension of himself, a tool that he wielded with the same precision as his earlier days operating machinery deep within the Earth's crust. Today, however, the minerals and metals beneath the surface were not his focus; it was the ground itself, the very land that had been excavated and now yearned for restoration.

"Land reclamation," he began, his voice carrying the weight of responsibility. "Is not merely about returning the land to its former state. It is about stewardship, about engineering a future where the environment and our industries can coexist sustainably."

He clicked to the next slide, showcasing a barren landscape on the left transitioning into a thriving green space on the right. His fingers traced the lines of topography on the screen as if he could feel the texture of the earth through the pixels.

"Here, we have a before-and-after scenario at the Obotan mine site." Emeka's accent, seasoned by continents, lent gravity to his words. "The challenge was not only to fill the voids left behind but to ensure the soil's integrity for future generations. We implemented a multi-tiered strategy involving soil amelioration, hydroseeding, and community-led agricultural initiatives."

As Emeka explained how compaction and grading worked, it was clear he loved what he did. This wasn't just a job to him; it showed how much he believed engineering could help fix problems caused by mining. He shared charts, numbers, and plans, but it was his strong belief in what he was saying that really touched the audience. His belief came from many years of experience in different places and learning from different cultures.

With each slide, Emeka painted a picture of possibility, of landscapes reborn under the careful watch of those who dared to dream of balance between human ambition and nature's grace.

Emeka clicked the remote, and the screen faded to black. Silence preceded the swell of applause that cascaded through the conference room, and the collective clapped a rhythmic testament to his eloquence and expertise. He nodded in acknowledgment, allowing himself the briefest moment of pride. The questions came like a gentle rain, but he met them with ease, his answers concise, informed by years of hands-on work.

As the session wound down, Emeka collected his notes, feeling the weight of their satisfaction in the air, a subtle buoyancy lifting the corners of his lips. It was as if a gentle breeze was lifting the corners of his lips.

"Care for a cup of coffee?" Peter, one of the managers from the presentation, asked him, extending a hand and smiling warmly.

"Sure." Emeka smiled and followed

"How did you like the presentation?" Emeka asked as they sat down with their coffee in hand.

"You did well." Stirring creamer into his steaming cup, the manager's gaze held respect, a reflection of shared professional camaraderie. "Your technical knowledge—it's impressive. But if I may—" He hesitated just enough to be polite. "Perhaps consider a softer sell on the stats and figures. Canadians connect with stories, the human element. It's about painting a picture they can see themselves in."

"Thank you," Emeka said, absorbing the advice like the rich aroma of the dark roast in his hand. "I'll keep that in mind for next time. The narrative is indeed powerful."

They sipped their drinks in silence before Peter leaned in, his smile lingering with a hint of curiosity.

"Emeka," he began, tilting his head slightly, "where are you from? I could not place your accent; it is not fully Nigerian, is it?"

At that moment, the myriad of places that had shaped Emeka seemed to echo in his mind – the bustling streets of Lagos, the misty lochs of Scotland, the sun-scorched expanse of Australia, and finally, the crisp air *of Canada. His journey was etched into the very way the words left his mouth, a tapestry of cultures woven through his diction.*

Code-switching is an important phenomenon in the complicated world of language and identity, particularly for immigrants adjusting to new cultural contexts. Although code-switching frequently entails changing between languages, it can also apply specifically to the process of altering speech patterns or accents in order to blend in with different social situations. This ability enables people to move through various settings without losing their identity.

For many immigrants, code-switching becomes a necessary tool for integration. Upon arriving in a new country, individuals may encounter a diverse array of accents and dialects that can significantly influence how they are perceived. A strong accent from their native country may lead to misconceptions about their capabilities or intelligence. In contrast, adopting a more neutral or local accent can facilitate smoother interactions and help reduce the likelihood of discrimination.

This adaptability is not merely a linguistic exercise; it is deeply tied to identity and survival. For instance, an immigrant may naturally slip into a local accent when conversing with colleagues or friends while reverting to their original accent when speaking with family or members of their ethnic community. This duality allows them to navigate their new world while maintaining a connection to their cultural roots (Abdul-Zahra, 2010).

The reasons behind accent code-switching are multifaceted. Many individuals feel the pressure to conform to the accent norms of their environment, believing that doing so will enhance their social acceptance and professional opportunities. This shift can foster a sense of belonging, making it easier for immigrants to feel integrated into their new communities. However, it can also create an internal conflict as individuals grapple with the fear of losing their cultural identity in the process.

Furthermore, the social dynamics of power are frequently reflected in the practice of accent change. People who can modify their speech patterns to conform to the norms of the prevailing culture could be given more opportunities and respect. On the other hand, people who are unable or unwilling to change their accents may encounter obstacles that prevent them from succeeding and being accepted (Nurmia & Koroma, 2020).

In essence, accent code-switching illustrates the intricate interplay between language, culture, and identity. It highlights how individuals navigate the challenges of integration while striving to honor their heritage. As we explore the impact of accents on perceptions of immigrants, it becomes clear that code-switching is not merely a linguistic choice; it is a vital strategy for connection and survival in an ever-evolving world.

Our voices bear the imprints of our history, culture, and experiences. The way we curl our tongues around words, the rhythm and pitch of our speech - all these elements form a unique melody that tells a tale about us. Often overlooked, accents are powerful symbols of identity that influence how others perceive us in both personal and professional spheres.

Accents are a symphony of linguistic features, each adding its own note to the grand orchestra of communication. "Out of the world's approximately 7.8 billion inhabitants, 1.35 billion speak English. The majority aren't native English speakers, however. About 360 million people speak English as their first language" (Lyons, 2021). This diversity is a testament to the depth of linguistic variety, where even slight changes in pronunciation can reveal significant information about one's background.

Consider Received Pronunciation (RP), often seen as the epitome of British accents due to its clear enunciation. Only about 3-5% of the UK population speaks with this accent associated with higher education and social status. Its perceived superiority can impact social mobility as individuals with RP accents may be viewed as more authoritative or educated (Luzzi, 2020).

In contrast, East London's Cockney accent is richly textured and vibrant. Known for its unique vowel shifts and colloquial phrases like "apples and pears" for "stairs," it offers a window into the cultural richness of London's working-class roots. Accents such as Cockney serve not only as markers of identity but also face societal biases.

From continent to continent, accents continue to shape perceptions. The Australian accent characterized by elongated vowels lends everyday words like "mate" and "day" a laid-back cadence reflective of Australia's relaxed lifestyle. With over 70% speaking English at home, according to Australian Bureau Statistics, this distinct accent becomes an integral part of national identity (Australian Bureau Statistics, 2016).

The Indian English accent has a unique sound, like turning "table" into "teh-buhl." It often reflects the patterns of local languages, which makes it an interesting mix of different influences. Studies show that these differences can help people from different backgrounds feel more connected (Kirkpatrick, 2010).

The Arabic English accent offers a playful exchange between "p" and "b," transforming words like "pat" into "bat." This accent carries cultural significance, reflecting the linguistic heritage of Arabic speakers while navigating English's intricacies (British Accent Academy.com).

The South African English accent offers a delightful blend of British and Afrikaans influences. The way "pen" sounds like "pin" illustrates how regional variations can reshape language. Yet, this accent still grapples with the legacy of apartheid, where accents were tied to social status and privilege. (Goatley-Soan & Baldwin, 2018).

Then there's the Latin American English accent, which infuses Spanish influence into its speech. Words are pronounced with clearer vowels, creating a melodious tonality. For instance, "thank you" may sound like "tank you," reflecting the speaker's linguistic heritage. The rhythmic quality of this accent can evoke warmth and expressiveness, enhancing interpersonal relationships and cultural exchanges.

Lastly, African English accents weave a vibrant tapestry of influences. In Nigeria, for example, local idioms enrich the accent, showcasing cultural pride. Words like "ask" can be pronounced as "aks," echoing many African languages' rhythmic cadence (Blog - Brenda, 2020).

Accents shape social dynamics and professional opportunities significantly. Standard accents like RP in the UK or General American in the US are often linked to authority and professionalism, providing social advantages, including better job prospects while some accents carry negative stereotypes hindering social mobility.

The charm of an accent is deeply personal, depending on the listener's background and context. Accents can foster a sense of belonging, but they also serve as barriers reinforcing societal divisions. Appreciating the diversity of accents is vital for fostering inclusivity and dismantling stereotypes.

English Class

Mr. Patel cleared his throat before he started teaching. His dark, smart eyes looked over the students—some excited, some not so interested—while he put a hand on a pile of old books on his desk. The smell of chalk from past lessons mixed with the usual teenage smell that filled the 8th-grade English classroom.

"Good morning, class," he said, his voice rich with the melodic lilt of his Indian heritage. He could sense the effort his vocal cords made to twist around the vowels, to harden the consonants in ways familiar to his students yet foreign to his tongue. "Today, we shall embark upon a journey through the realms of metaphor and allegory."

He turned to the blackboard, where the chalk etched his thoughts into existence. Each letter was meticulously crafted despite the accent within his mind that sometimes made even the written word feel like an uncharted landscape.

"Can anyone give me an example of a metaphor from your readings last night?" Mr. Patel asked, turning back to face the sea of desks. His gaze swept over the students, noting the mosaic of cultures represented in Luton's small-town school—the bright headscarves, the variety of skin tones ranging from milky to deep brown, each a testament to the diversity threading through the fabric of English society.

"Remember," he continued, the smile lines at the corners of his eyes deepening, "language is not just a tool for communication but an art form."

He rested his head on his desk's edge. His easy yet authoritative stance was reinforced in silence by the authority of his Ph.D. in English literature. He was well acquainted with the classics that adorned the bookshelves, each spine serving as a companion in his enduring passion for words. However, in this classroom, it was more than just the facts he taught; it was also about bridging the gap between his world and theirs, one word at a time, with careful pronunciation.

A slender hand shot up from the third row, a hesitant voice wavering through the air. "Mr. Patel, could you please say that again?" The girl's eyes were apologetic, her shoulders slightly hunched.

"Of course," Mr. Patel replied with an encouraging nod, repeating his earlier question on metaphors. He articulated each syllable with deliberate precision, his tongue a cautious negotiator between his thoughts and their expression.

"Sorry, but I still didn't get it. Could you, um, try one more time?" she asked, biting her lip as though she were the one inconveniencing him rather than the other way around.

With patience born of years navigating such moments, Mr. Patel obliged once more, his accent curling around the words like a gentle embrace. He scanned the room, seeking signs of comprehension, hoping his passion for the subject would bridge the linguistic divide.

Then, from the back of the classroom, a boy's query cut through the tentative silence that had fallen over the students. "Why don't you speak English like everybody else?" There was no malice in his tone, just pure, unfiltered curiosity, the kind that children often possess before the world teaches them the intricacies of tact.

For a time, Mr. Patel felt the weight of his accent more vividly than ever, a faint shadow across his assurance. He did not, however, allow the sentiment to persist. Rather, a warm smile returned to his face as he straightened his back.

"Language," he began, addressing the entire class now, "is as varied as the people who use it. Just like our fingerprints, each person's way of speaking is unique. My accent tells a story of where I have been, what I have learned, and the many places I call home." His voice held steady, a calm sea of resolve amidst the undercurrents of self-consciousness.

"Understanding someone's different way of speaking," he continued, "Can teach us a lot about acceptance and the beauty of diversity in our world. It's very much like appreciating different genres of literature—it broadens our horizons, wouldn't you agree?"

At that moment, it wasn't just English literature that Mr. Patel was teaching. It was empathy, tolerance, and the quiet strength that comes from knowing who you are.

The path to assimilation into the North American cultural mosaic is a labyrinthine journey for immigrants, where accents don unique and layered roles. These phonetic signatures impact every facet of life, from educational experiences, professional engagements, and social interactions to emotional health. Accents are an integral part of linguistic diversity, but they can shape how individuals view themselves and how they are seen by others in powerful ways.

For many immigrants, an accent is not just how they speak; it's a strong symbol of their cultural background. It connects them to where they come from and reflects their personal and shared history. But this connection can also bring challenges. An accent can make them stand out, affecting how they interact with others and how accepted they feel in new places.

Numerous studies reveal that those with distinct accents frequently encounter stereotypes and biases that imply inferior competence or intelligence. Research suggests that speakers with non-native English accents might be viewed as less professional or less capable, irrespective of their actual credentials This perception can pose hurdles for immigrants trying to form bonds and blend into local communities. The dread of judgment can turn everyday conversations into intimidating tasks, erecting barriers to social interaction (Huang, Frideger & Pearce, 2014).

In academic settings, accents can introduce unique obstacles. Students with marked accents may find it hard to communicate effectively with educators and classmates, leading to miscommunications and social seclusion. For instance, a Chinese student studying in Canada might struggle to express complex ideas in English, resulting in frustration and alienation. One article states that more than 40% of students confessed feeling embarrassed about their accents in class which led to decreased participation and diminished sense of belonging the classroom, a place meant for growth and learning, can morph into a source of anxiety when an accent becomes a hurdle to acceptance (Coppinger & Sheridan, 2022).

In professional settings, accents can muddle relationships. Immigrants might find that their accents sway hiring choices and opportunities for career progression. Research by the Harvard Business Review discovered the native speakers were, on average, 16% likelier to be recommended for the job even when qualifications were identical. This bias can erect barriers that are tough to surmount (Huang, Frideger & Pearce, 2014).

Misunderstandings stemming from accents can lead to miscommunications between colleagues, causing frustration and further seclusion. The pressure to conform to "standard" speech patterns may push immigrants to modify their accents in an attempt to fit in, creating internal conflict and possibly diluting their connection to their cultural identity.

The emotional strain of navigating life with a noticeable accent can be significant. Many immigrants find themselves trapped in a struggle between preserving their cultural identity and integrating into a new environment. This tension often leads to feelings of anxiety, depression, and identity crisis. According to the Journal of World Business, immigrants who feel alienated due to their accents are at higher risk for mental health issues, with studies showing increased levels of stress and lower life satisfaction (Nurmia & Koroma, 2020).

For instance, a recent immigrant from India might feel pressured to alter their accent to avoid judgment, which can create a sense of loss regarding their cultural identity. The ensuing internal discord can manifest as emotional turmoil as they grapple with the desire for acceptance while also wanting to honor their heritage.

Despite these challenges, though, the journey toward assimilation is often marked by resilience and adaptability. Immigrants often develop strategies to navigate their linguistic landscape, finding ways to embrace their accents while also seeking to connect with others. Their stories underscore the dual role of accents as both hurdles and bridges to their culture and community.

For example, many immigrants actively participate in cultural exchange, where they educate others about their backgrounds while also learning about their new environment. This mutual exchange fosters understanding and acceptance, creating richer social interactions. Communities that celebrate linguistic diversity can help alleviate some of the pressures associated with accent-based discrimination.

The interplay of accents, identity, and the immigrant experience is intricate and multi-layered. As individuals traverse this complex terrain, they reflect on their relationships, aspirations, and sense of belonging. Their narratives are rich with resilience, revealing how accents—while often perceived as barriers—also symbolize deep connections to culture and community. The challenges and triumphs associated with accents are vital parts of the immigrant experience, underscoring the diverse stories that enrich the cultural fabric of North American society. By fostering understanding and appreciation for this diversity, we can work towards a more inclusive and accepting society.

Chapter Five - Culture Part I: The Great Divide

"A nation's culture resides in the hearts and in the soul of its people."

- Mahatma Gandhi

Work and Play

John Smith cast a quick glance at the clock on his computer screen, a small smile of satisfaction gracing his lips as the digits marched steadily toward the end of another productive day. With a contented sigh, he stretched his arms above his head and swiveled in his chair to face the cluster of cubicles where his colleagues were beginning to wind down their work and engage in casual banter.

"Hey, folks!" John called out, his voice embodying the very essence of Friday—easygoing, relaxed, a precursor to the weekend ahead. "Anyone up for grabbing some drinks? My treat for the first round."

A ripple of enthusiasm surged through the office like an electric current. Chairs rolled back with muted wheels, and screens flickered off as the team began to coalesce around the idea, drawn together by a magnetic force of camaraderie. It was more than just an after-work gathering; it was a ritual of unwinding, a shared moment that often transformed mere co-workers into genuine companions.

"Sounds like a plan," echoed one of the developers, effortlessly slinging her bag over her shoulder. Another person suggested a new place downtown, famous for its amazing rooftop views and special handmade drinks. Everyone was excited about the evening ahead, making the lively atmosphere even more fun.

Amidst the constant chatter and clattering of keyboards, Ahmed Khan sat at his desk, his computer humming softly in contrast to the rising tide of conversation. He couldn't help but admire John's effortless way of bringing people together, a skill that seemed just as natural to him as coding did to Ahmed. It was a quality that made John a focal point within the team's social structure.

As the group began to disperse towards the exit, the symphony of clicking locks and shuffling papers set the rhythm for their departure. John, always inclusive, shot a knowing look over to Ahmed, silently inviting him to join. "Come on, man," one of their colleagues nudged with a grin, catching Ahmed's eye. "Don't leave us drinking alone."

Ahmed offered a polite smile in response, but his words were lost in the swell of laughter and footsteps as his team made their way out into the evening. He watched them filter out, one by one, a colorful mosaic of individuals united by the simple act of sharing time beyond office walls.

The neon glow of the exit sign flickered above as Sarah Miller turned back from the threshold, her silhouette framed by the fading light of the office. The hum of Ahmed's dual monitors was punctuated by the sound of her voice calling out to him. She stood in the doorway, beckoning him with a warm smile and an outstretched hand.

"Hey Ahmed," she called across to him, her voice breaking through the quiet. "You should come with us."

Ahmed's fingers paused mid-stroke on the keyboard. The cursor blinked expectantly as he turned to meet her gaze. Her eyes sparkled with kindness, and she smiled. She was extending an olive branch, inviting him to be a part of their team's camaraderie.

"John found this cool spot downtown," she continued, tucking a strand of hair behind her ear. "It's casual, just some drinks to cap off the week. What do you say?"

Despite her warmth and sincerity, Ahmed felt a knot form in his stomach at the mention of alcohol. In Pakistan, social gatherings were centered around family and shared meals, not drinking — a boundary dictated not only by personal preference but also by his faith.

For a moment, Ahmed's eyes darted away, seeking refuge in the familiar stack of codebooks on his desk before he mustered the courage to look at Sarah again.

"Thank you for the invitation, Sarah," he said carefully, weighing his words. "But I think I will pass tonight."

There was a softness in his tone that betrayed the internal struggle he faced. He offered a placid smile, hoping it would bridge the cultural gap without further explanation.

As Sarah's own smile faltered, Ahmed could see disappointment in her eyes. He felt a pang of guilt, knowing that, once again, his culture and beliefs had created a divide between him and his colleagues. But he couldn't compromise his values for the sake of fitting in.

"Are you sure?" Sarah asked, her voice laced with concern.

Ahmed nodded, trying to convey his gratitude for the invitation without causing any offense. "I'm sure," he replied softly.

Sarah sighed, her shoulders slumping slightly. "Well, maybe another time," she said before turning to leave.

Watching her walk away, Ahmed couldn't help but feel a sense of isolation wash over him. He was well aware that his devoutness often set him apart from those around him, but it still hurt when it led to moments like this – being left out of social gatherings or feeling like an outsider in his own workplace.

He turned back to his computer screen, trying to focus on the lines of code in front of him. But all he could think about was how different things were back home in Pakistan. There, he had never felt like an outsider among his friends and family. They all shared similar values and traditions, creating a tight-knit community where he belonged.

But here in America, Ahmed often found himself struggling to find that same sense of connection. The cultural differences were vast and, at *times, overwhelming — especially when it came to something as simple as going out for drinks with coworkers.*

In both work and social life, networking is very important. It's the foundation for building relationships and creating opportunities. But networking isn't the same everywhere; it works differently in each culture. Understanding these differences can help make conversations across cultures more successful and create strong connections. Let's explore how networking works in seven different countries: the USA, Canada, the UK, Australia, Japan, Russia, and Morocco. Each has its own way of doing things.

In the vibrant cities and towns of America, networking flourishes on a casual and direct approach. Americans appreciate openness and candor, often engaging in light-hearted chatter over coffee or at networking gatherings. "80% of professionals find networking essential to their career success, almost 100% believe that face-to-face meetings build stronger long-term relationships, and 41% want to network more often" (Bradshaw, 2024).

During these exchanges, individuals usually reveal their interests openly and are prompt to share business cards, often within the initial moments of conversation. American culture underscores punctuality, with timely follow-ups seen as a sign of professionalism.

Crossing into Canada's borders, networking maintains an informal tone but is often laced with courtesy and warmth. Canadians favor a friendly approach where small talk precedes business discussions. Like their American counterparts, Canadians place a high priority on directness, but they also emphasize the significance of inclusivity and respect. In Canada, networking events usually attract a varied range of attendees, reflecting the nation's multiculturalism. Because of this dual strategy, networking events feel more like community get-togethers than transactional meetings, fostering an atmosphere where different viewpoints are valued (Blog-Canadian Networking Events).

In the United Kingdom, networking is marked by a mix of formality and professional grace. British networking demands impeccable etiquette, polite greetings and the usage of formal titles are customary. British individuals often favor subtlety over blatant self-promotion, valuing modesty in professional interactions. This preference can sometimes be seen as reticence by individuals from more direct cultures, but it's crucial to recognize that this approach stems from a desire to build genuine relationships based on mutual respect (Livermore, 2013).

Australia's networking landscape strikes a balance between friendliness and professionalism. Australians are known for their laid-back demeanor, which influences their networking style. Casual settings such as barbecues or social events are popular venues for networking.

Despite this relaxed approach, Australians appreciate clarity and honesty in discussions. Business cards are exchanged, but the focus often remains on building genuine relationships rather than merely transactional interactions. Networking in Australia often includes humor and a relaxed attitude, which can help ease initial awkwardness in conversations (Livermore, 2013).

In Japan, networking practices are deeply rooted in cultural values such as respect, hierarchy, and formality. Japanese networking is characterized by meticulous attention to etiquette. Business card exchanges, or "meishi," are formal affairs where cards are presented and received with both hands, signifying the importance of interaction (Takeri & Alston, 2018).

In the sun-drenched land of Morocco, the art of networking unfolds as a warm, hospitable dance choreographed by time-honored traditions. Here, personal bonds and respect for hierarchy are the life bloods of communication. Conversations meander like Moroccan rivers, first nurturing rapport before veering towards business matters.

Moroccan networking gatherings are a tapestry woven with both formal and informal threads. Hospitality is the loom on which this tapestry is created—sharing meals and drinks cultivates a sense of community and trust. Navigating these interactions requires a keen understanding of cultural norms like gender dynamics.

Storytelling also plays its part in Moroccan networking—a shared anecdote or personal experience can serve as a bridge between individuals. These narratives not only fortify relationships but also enrich conversations, offering deeper insight into one another's backgrounds and viewpoints (Livermore, 2013).

In contrast, networking in Russia combines formality with the development of strategic relationships. Boardrooms reverberate with formal introductions, and full names and titles are revered.

Establishing personal rapport is paramount—trust and credibility often sprout from the fertile ground of mutual acquaintances. Russian networking events might initially focus on the interpersonal connection before segueing into business discussions—a testament to the importance placed on relationships where deals are often sealed based on trust rather than solely contractual agreements.

The shadowy remnants of Soviet-era practices still linger in Russian business dynamics—personal relationships frequently trump formal structures. This historical context is crucial when navigating Russia's unique blend of traditional and contemporary practices in networking (Livermore, 2013).

In conclusion, networking norms are as diverse as the cultures they spring from—each reflecting their distinct values and social customs. While countries like America and Canada favor casual and direct approaches, the UK and Australia marry formality with friendliness. Japan, Russia, and Morocco lean towards their deep-seated cultural traditions that underscore respect, hierarchy, and relationship-building.

Recognizing these cultural subtleties is vital for effective networking and fruitful cross-cultural interactions. Adapting to local customs not only bolsters one's ability to foster meaningful professional ties but also nurtures a sense of respect and appreciation for diverse cultures. Embracing these differences allows individuals to traverse the intricate terrain of global networking with confidence and success—ultimately enriching both their personal and professional lives.

The Negotiation Table

The bright white conference room was only slightly softened by the afternoon sunlight coming through the tall windows. Outside, Moscow stretched out, mixing history and modern life, but inside the room, everything seemed to stop for the deal being made.

I sat, rigid yet poised, across from my Russian counterpart, Ivan—a man whose reputation preceded him. Our handshake had been firm, the brief pleasantries curt, as if words were mere formalities before the true conversation began. Ivan's eyes, sharp and assessing, met mine with a weight that acknowledged the gravity of our meeting.

"Mr. Adefulu," he said, his voice low and steady, "Shall we?"

"Indeed, Mr. Petrov," I replied, leaning forward slightly. The distance between us bristled with unspoken understanding; our respective companies' futures hinged on the outcome of our discussions.

Our first exchange was a careful dance. We delved into the matter at hand, the air growing thick with the tension of negotiation. There was no need for small talk—the figures and contracts scattered across the table spoke volumes more than any cordial chit-chat could offer.

The table before us transformed into an archipelago of paperwork, each island a testament to the asset's value—numbers, projections, and valuations vying for prominence. We were marooned amidst a sea of figures that churned and swelled with every page we turned, every line we scrutinized. Ivan's fingers traced columns of digits that spelled out not just monetary worth but strategic influence.

"Thirty percent over five years," I murmured, my eyes locked on the forecasted revenue stream. It was more than profit; it was a footprint in the snow, a marker of presence and power.

Ivan nodded slowly, his gaze never leaving the paper, the furrow between his brows deepening. "And distribution rights?" he queried, a subtle tilt of his head indicating the weight he placed on this particular detail.

"Exclusive," I responded, asserting the promise and potential our partnership held. For my company, this deal was a lodestone, set to draw us deeper into the Russian market—a place where roots could grow from transactions, where relationships could warm even the coldest Siberian business climate.

He leaned back, folding his arms as if to cradle the future of his company within them. A deep position in Russia for us, an entry point in the UK for them; our aspirations mirrored each other, two sides of the same coin spinning on the table of negotiations. Our companies were poised at the threshold of mutual advancement, and this deal was the key turning in the lock of opportunity.

"Your move into the UK," I ventured, watching the play of thoughts across Ivan's face. "Will redefine your company's global stance."

"Da," he acknowledged, his voice a low rumble, "And your company will secure its foothold here." The acknowledgment carried a weight of its own, bearing the gravity of decisions that would echo through boardrooms and across continents.

The numbers whispered secrets of success and growth, and we, their interpreters, were left to decode the language of commerce that would bind our companies in a dance of international synergy.

The stale air of the conference room seemed to thicken with tension, each tick of the clock on the wall stretching moments into eternities. Ivan's gaze remained fixed on the spreadsheet before him, his eyes tracing columns and rows that we had dissected ad nauseam. Across from him, I tapped a pen against the edge of the table, a rhythmic echo to the silence that had settled between us.

"Look, Ivan," I started, breaking the impasse, "We've been over these figures. The valuation is more than fair." My words hung in the space, bold yet hopeful, seeking common ground in a landscape marred by discord.

He glanced up, his expression unreadable as he shuffled the papers, the sound crinkling through the stalemate. "I agree the numbers are accurate," he finally said, his voice betraying no hint of concession. "But there is something... not quite aligning with our vision."

I let out a slow breath, sensing the tension building between us, making the agreement feel harder to reach. It was like two strong forces clashing, and in that moment, the chance for partnership was being held back by an invisible challenge.

"Then let's revisit the vision," I suggested, leaning forward, determined to find the thread that would unravel the deadlock. "Our companies have so much to gain from this."

"Perhaps." He closed the folder with a soft snap—a definitive end to today's discourse. "But for now, we pause."

My chair scraped against the floor as I stood, the sound jarring in contrast to the unresolved quiet. We exchanged curt nods, a mutual acknowledgment of the impasse, and I gathered my documents, my movements brusque, driven by a storm of frustration brewing within.

The Moscow Twilight greeted me with its customary chill as I exited the building, the city's vibrant energy mocking my own sense of defeat. The drive back to the hotel was a blur of lights and shadow, reflections of my own internal turmoil.

Alone in the elevator's ascent, the mirrored walls reflected a man whose determination was edged with doubt. Was it really just the deal that Ivan wasn't warming to? My mind wrestled with the question but provided no solace.

Back in the sanctuary of my hotel room, I loosened my tie with a sigh, the fabric's constraint a metaphor for the day's negotiations. I knew, without a shred of doubt, that our offer was equitable, the opportunity ripe. Yet Ivan, my counterpart, remained a bastion of resistance—unyielding and inscrutable.

With my hands deep in my pockets, I stood at the window and looked out over the skyline of Moscow. Only the harshness of artificial light could direct my thoughts as the city's glow obscured the stars. The disappointment weighed heavily on my shoulders in the darkness, the day's failure a silent companion that echoed the chorus of missed opportunities and stagnant development.

Descending from my room to the hotel bar, the soft hum of conversation and the clink of glasses offered a soothing backdrop to my churning thoughts. I claimed a secluded corner booth; its leather embrace was a welcome change from the rigid lines of the conference room chairs. A waiter glided over, pad in hand, ready to take my order.

"Could I have the Borscht, please, and a glass of the house red?" I requested, trying to sound more at ease than I felt.

As she nodded and walked away, I leaned back against the cushioned seat, my gaze drifting across the dimly lit expanse of the bar. Patrons laughed and chatted, their faces illuminated by the flickering candles on each table. Their easy camaraderie seemed a world away from the impasse Ivan and I had faced just hours before.

I began to ponder if, perhaps, there was an element I had overlooked, a personal angle that hadn't yet surfaced. Could it be that it wasn't the figures and facts of the deal itself but something less tangible between us that had halted progress?

A momentary smile crossed my face, spurred by a newfound curiosity about the human part of business—a facet I had disregarded in my pursuit of a signed deal. With a subtle elegance that defied the late hour, the waitress came back and placed my food down.

"Excuse me," I ventured, capturing her attention. "What would you say is the best way to really get to know someone?"

She paused, a hint of surprise flashing across her features before she responded with a thoughtful tilt of her head. Her smile broadened as if pleased by the unexpected depth of the question amidst the routine of her shift.

"Like on a date?" Her voice held a playful lilt, perhaps misconstruing the depth of my earlier question.

I chuckled, shaking my head slightly. "No, no. More like...as friends, let's say." There was a vulnerability in admitting that what I sought was a genuine connection rather than a strategic business play.

She leaned against the bar, the light from above casting a soft glow on her face as she considered my clarification. "Friends, huh?" She smiled a gesture that seemed to carry a hint of shared understanding. "Then you should go out for a night on the town. Drink some vodka and share stories. It's how we do it here in Moscow. Nothing breaks the ice like a good toast and tales from the heart."

Her suggestion was a beacon in the fog that had clouded my mind since the stalemate at the negotiation table. It wasn't just about the deal; it was about understanding the man sitting across from me, Ivan, with his stoic demeanor and unreadable eyes. Perhaps sharing something beyond the dry numbers and projections could pave the way to mutual trust—and a breakthrough.

"Thank you," I said, a newfound optimism threading through my voice. "That might be just what I need."

As she nodded and turned away, her advice lingered in the air, mingling with the scent of rich food and the subtle notes of jazz playing softly in the background. Tonight, I had come looking for solace in the solitude of my thoughts, but instead, I found the prospect of camaraderie in an unfamiliar city. It was a strategy worth exploring, one that might just turn the tides in my favor.

The next morning, with the frosty light of Moscow threading through the blinds of my hotel room, I rehearsed the invitation in my head. As I met Ivan in the stark lobby of his corporate headquarters, the aroma of strong coffee did little to settle my nerves. I cleared my throat, extending the olive branch.

"Ivan, how about we take this evening off the paperwork? Would you join me for a drink tonight, maybe show me a bit of Moscow?"

Ivan's eyes, usually as hard as the frozen pavements outside softened into a look of mild surprise. A slight nod followed, "Yes, I would like that."

The city revealed itself under the cloak of night, not through the glaring lights of landmarks but in the warm glow of streetlamps and the buzz of life that echoed down its avenues. Ivan led me through a labyrinth of streets, each one with its own rhythm and story. We found ourselves at a bar that pulsed with the heartbeats of many past conversations, its walls steeped in layers of laughter and confessions.

Drinks clinked, and liquid fire coursed through our veins, loosening tongues and erasing borders. The tales spilled between us, laced with the flavors of vodka—smooth, sharp, and sincere. Ivan spoke of his children, the pride clear in his voice even as it wavered with the weight of responsibility.

"Two daughters," he said, raising his glass slightly before taking another sip. "They are the stars in my sky."

"Same here," I replied, warmth spreading through me, not all from the alcohol. "Two kids waiting for me back home."

We ventured further into personal territories, anecdotes of our respective travels painting a picture of lives constantly on the move, both of us charting pathways across countries for the sake of our work. It was a dance of words and shared experiences, a mutual understanding that began to bridge the gap widened by boardroom battles.

The night deepened around us, yet the connection felt strangely light, unburdened by the earlier tension. In that space, with the city humming its nocturnal tune, we discovered common ground beyond the numbers and the negotiations—a foundation built on the simple yet profound realization that, despite the miles and cultures between us, we weren't all that different after all.

The soft buzz of conversation faded into the background as Ivan leaned forward, his gaze more intent than before. The dim light of the bar cast shadows across his face, giving him a contemplative look. He swirled the remnants of his drink, ice cubes clinking against the glass.

"Tell me," Ivan began, his voice low and steady, "In your time in the UK... have you ever felt the sting of discrimination because of your skin color?"

I paused, the question hanging heavily in the air between us. It was not something I expected to discuss with Ivan, but the sincerity in his eyes encouraged honesty. My fingers played with the condensation on my own glass as I gathered my thoughts.

"Sometimes," I admitted the word escaping with a weight of its own. "It's not overt, but it's there—a look, a comment, an assumption."

Ivan nodded as he processed what I had said, a tacit understanding moving between us. His attentive attention elevated our discourse above mere bar chitchat. This was about recognizing and appreciating one other's humanity, not only about cultural exchanges.

When we parted ways that night, the frosty Moscow air felt less biting, as if our newfound camaraderie had granted us a shield against the cold.

The next day, as we re-entered the conference room, there was a palpable shift in the atmosphere. Our discussions moved with newfound fluidity—each concession and compromise smoothed over by the understanding we had fostered. The deal that seemed insurmountable just days before now progressed with an ease that surprised us both.

In sharing our vulnerabilities, we found strength. In acknowledging our common humanity, we paved the way for collaboration. As we shook hands over the final agreement, it was clear that the night spent under Moscow's expansive skies had done more than just break the ice—it had melted away the barriers to our success.

Coffee Break and Hockey

Yuliana sat at the edge of the breakroom table. Her fingers curled around a steaming cup of coffee that did little to ward off the chill seeping through the office windows. The chatter around her swelled as her colleagues, a close-knit team who navigated the ebbs and flows of their Winnipeg workspace like family, animatedly discussed the upcoming Thanksgiving dinner. The sound of their voices brought a sense of comfort to this new place she called home.

"Can't wait for the turkey this year," one of them declared, rubbing his hands together in anticipation. "And the stuffing! My wife's secret recipe is to die for."

Another colleague chimed in, "I'm all about the pumpkin pie. You can't have Thanksgiving without pumpkin pie." Their faces lit up with fond memories, and Yuliana couldn't help but feel a twinge of longing for her own family traditions back in Cali, Columbia.

They shared an easy camaraderie that spoke of years spent within these walls, a stark contrast to Yuliana's own burgeoning sense of belonging. She couldn't help but feel like a fledgling amidst seasoned birds, her memories of Cali, Columbia still vivid—a city pulsating with life and warmth that defied its chaos. Winnipeg was quieter, its rhythms slower, and she was still learning its dance.

It had been a year since she and her husband had packed their lives into suitcases, whispering hopeful goodbyes to a home that could no longer promise them a future. They sought refuge in this distant land where winter's breath lingered even in spring and where people spoke of holidays she had only seen depicted on television screens.

"Yuliana, right?" The voice pulled her from her reverie, and she nodded, offering a small, tentative smile. "What do you guys usually eat for Thanksgiving down in Columbia?"

She hesitated, the realization dawning that Thanksgiving was not a tradition in her native land. "Well, we don't celebrate Thanksgiving in Columbia, but we have other holidays where we come together with our families and share a meal like Día de la Independencia." She could almost taste her grandmother's home-cooked meals as she spoke.

Her colleagues listened, intrigued, as she recounted tales of bandeja paisa brimming with flavors and the music that felt like a second language to her people. She painted a vivid picture of vibrant colors and laughter, describing her grandmother's hands expertly preparing ajiaco.

"Sounds wonderful," one of her colleagues murmured, and Yuliana felt a flicker of pride. Her story had given her a voice in this circle, and while she was yet a stranger to the customs here, perhaps there was room at the table for her tales, too.

"So, what's typically served at Thanksgiving here?" she asked, her accent wrapping around the words like a soft embrace.

"Turkey's the main star," replied one colleague, his eyes lighting up. "Mashed potatoes, gravy, and oh, you can't forget about the stuffing and cranberry sauce." The thought of all these dishes combined made Yuliana's mouth water.

"Sounds delicious," Yuliana mused, imagining the warmth such a meal would bring to the frosty Winnipeg evenings. She entertained the thought of hosting her own version of Thanksgiving dinner, blending the flavors of her heritage with this newfound tradition. The idea of inviting some colleagues over danced in her mind, a gesture to bridge the gap between her past and present life. But before she could voice her intentions, the conversation took an unexpected turn. "Hey, did everyone hear? The boss is planning to get us tickets for the next Jets game!" another colleague interjected enthusiastically. A wave of excitement rippled through the group as they eagerly made plans for the game.

Excitement bubbled within the group, their voices eager and animated as they discussed the intricacies of hockey. Yolanda sat among them, trying to keep up with the flurry of terms being thrown around like snowflakes in a blizzard—beautiful but bewildering. She couldn't help but feel a mixture of fascination and confusion at their passionate discussion on power plays and penalty kills.

As they talked more about hockey, Yuliana kept smiling, even though she quietly thought about her Thanksgiving invitation. She knew she would have time to think about Canadian food later. For now, she just listened, taking in the excitement and energy of the local sports culture from her colleagues, who were all hoping to get tickets to a game.

The laughter and cheers around the table grew louder, building to a crescendo as they all envisioned themselves in the stands together. One colleague clapped another on the back, their eyes alight with camaraderie. "It's going to be epic," they exclaimed, "nothing beats experiencing a live game with the electric atmosphere in the arena!"

"Especially when it goes into overtime," added another with a broad grin. "The tension, the cheers, and then the collective roar when we score—it's pure adrenaline!"

Yuliana nodded along, her lips curving into a polite smile that she hoped conveyed shared enthusiasm. She watched as one colleague *pantomimed a player's slapshot, his arms swooping through the air while his colleagues responded with approving laughter.*

Inside, though, Yuliana couldn't shake off a twinge of disconnect. The terminology was foreign to her, the rules arcane. She had caught glimpses of the sport on television screens before but had never fully understood its complexities.

She appreciated the invitation to partake in a cherished Canadian pastime and be included in this ritual that clearly meant so much to her new friends. Yet the thought of sitting amidst a roaring crowd, straining to decipher the intricacies of hockey, left her feeling adrift in a sea of unfamiliarity.

The conversation shifted as one of the colleagues turned towards Yuliana, idly spinning a puck-shaped stress ball in his hand. "Hey, Yuliana," he said with an easy grin that suggested camaraderie, "Who's your favorite hockey team?"

Her heart skipped a beat, and she felt all eyes on her. At that moment, the distance between Cali and Winnipeg seemed to stretch even further. She fixed a warm but cautious smile on her face and replied with a hopeful lilt in her voice, "Oh, the local team, of course."

Laughter and nods of approval circled the table as someone chimed in enthusiastically about the team's recent winning streak. Yuliana let out a silent sigh of relief, her polite smile never wavering as she silently thanked her husband for mentioning the city's hockey pride just the other night. She made a mental note to ask him to explain the offside rule—a term that had floated past her several times during this very conversation.

The art of networking is a fundamental pillar in both our professional and social spheres, serving as the bedrock for relationship-building, idea exchange, and opportunity creation. Sports, however, offer an even more versatile and universal platform for connection. They are not just games; they are a global dialect of fervor and rivalry, deeply entwined with cultural identities and societal dynamics worldwide. The impact of sports on culture surfaces in countless ways—from fostering unity within communities and national pride to promoting personal growth and facilitating international interactions.

Take Brazil as an example, where football is far beyond a leisure activity—it's an all-consuming passion that unites the nation. The excitement that engulfs football matches breaks down economic and racial walls, creating a common sense of belonging among fans. "In addition, before the Confederations Cup and World Cup FIFA 2014, a survey conducted by the Brazilian Institute of Statistics and Public Opinion in 2013 revealed that 77% of Brazilian people consider football the biggest Brazilian passion" (Tobar & Gusso, 2017).

The World Cup becomes an arena for collective national pride as millions unite to cheer for their teams. However, this overpowering enthusiasm can often feel exclusive for immigrants. While locals revel in their teams' victories with zealous friendship, newcomers may find it difficult to fit in—struggling with both adapting to a new culture and understanding the unwritten rules of a sport that tends to favor familiarity.

Additionally, traditional sports serve as cultural pillars. Wrestling, a long-standing sport in Mongolia, is exhibited at the Naadam Festival. In addition to showcasing athletic prowess, this event honors cultural history and ideals like respect and honor. Similar to this, kabaddi in India represents strategy and teamwork, which has a deep impact on the communities that play it. By taking part in these events, community members can develop a sense of pride while also preserving cultural traditions. As people apply the values they have acquired from sports to their professional lives, this cultural pride frequently permeates encounters at work, encouraging collaboration and respect among coworkers.

In the United States, the National Football League (NFL) enjoys immense popularity, with its championship game—the Super Bowl—is one of the most watched sporting events annually. According to Nielsen, the 2022 Super Bowl attracted over 100 million viewers, marking it as a significant cultural event (Nielsen, 2022). Football games transcend mere sports; they come with tailgating, halftime shows, and community gatherings that strengthen social bonds. Yet, for an immigrant, these communal celebrations can feel isolating. While others connect over shared experiences at the game, newcomers may find themselves on the outskirts—struggling to comprehend not just the game but also its deeper cultural significance.

Moreover, sports in the U.S. play a crucial role in networking within professional circles. Many organizations use sports to foster teamwork and camaraderie among employees through team-building exercises inspired by sports, such as company-sponsored games or fitness challenges. For an immigrant, though, participating in these activities can be a double-edged sword—an opportunity to engage and connect but also a reminder of cultural nuances they may not fully understand.

The National Hockey League (NHL), particularly popular in Canada and northern U.S. states, showcases fierce competition during the Stanley Cup playoffs. Celebrated for its speed and physicality, hockey has a strong grassroots presence in youth leagues across North America. According to Hockey Canada, over 350,000 children participate in organized hockey each year (Hockey Canada, 2021). The shared passion for this sport fosters robust community ties that often translate into workplace camaraderie. However, immigrants may feel detached as they navigate not only the sport itself but also broader cultural dynamics at play—for instance, understanding why playoff games are so intense can be intimidating for someone unfamiliar with the sport or its significance in Canadian culture.

Sports like volleyball also play a vital role in cultural identity, with significant followings in countries such as China and the Philippines. The Philippine National Volleyball Team boasts a passionate fan base, with the sport being an integral part of school and community activities. According to Asia News Network "Volleyball is now the number one sport among spectators in the Philippines" (Lance Agcaoili-Philippine Daily Inquirer, 2024).

Similarly, in China, volleyball has gained international acclaim, particularly with the success of its women's national team. These sports promote teamwork and resilience—qualities equally valued in professional settings.

Yet, for someone new to these environments, understanding cultural references and insider knowledge can lead to feelings of exclusion. Networking through sports in these countries might involve different expectations and behaviors—creating obstacles for immigrants trying to integrate into local customs and practices.

The reach of sports goes beyond shaping cultural identities and promoting community ties; it significantly influences work interactions as well. Informal gatherings centered around sporting events can break down hierarchical barriers—creating opportunities for open dialogue among employees and management.

However, if one feels disconnected from the celebrated sport, these gatherings can feel more like reminders of one's outsider status than chances for integration. This dichotomy illustrates the complexities of using sports as a networking tool—it can bring people together but also highlight differences.

In conclusion, sports' influence on culture and work interactions is profound. As a medium for connection, sports foster community bonds and instill values that enhance teamwork and collaboration within professional environments. However, for immigrants—the experience can be mixed—while sports have the potential to bridge cultural divides—they can also serve as reminders of the complexities of belonging. By navigating these dynamics, both newcomers and established community members can contribute to a richer, more inclusive narrative that celebrates diversity in passion and competition.

Chapter Six- Culture Part II: The Unspoken Dialogue

"To truly connect with people from other cultures, one must understand not only their words but the silent language of their bodies."

- Unknown

City Lights and New Beginnings

The sleek car glided along the Gardiner Expressway, carrying Markos and Kulap towards a significant event. The Toronto skyline loomed ahead, its towering buildings glowing against the darkening sky like beacons, drawing them closer to its bustling heart.

Markos gripped the steering wheel tightly, his hands sweaty from nerves. He wiped them on his jeans without thinking, something he always did when he was anxious. Next to him, Kulap sat calmly, watching the cars move smoothly through traffic. The city was full of energy, so different from the quiet life she knew in Chiang Mai, Thailand. Still, she found it exciting. Her hands rested in her lap, and the engagement ring Markos had given her—a mix of Greek patterns and Thai gemstones—sparkled under the streetlights.

"We're almost there," Markos said, his voice tinged with excitement and a hint of anxiety that he couldn't quite conceal. His accent rolled the 'r' slightly, a comforting sound that always reminded Kulap of their first meeting in a charming coffee shop where the aroma of roasted beans mingled with the sweetness of her Thai iced tea.

"Do you think your family will like me?" Kulap asked softly, her voice barely audible over the hum of the car and the distant sounds of the city outside.

Markos glanced at her, noticing the slight furrow between her brows—a sure sign that she was lost in thought.

"They will love you," he reassured her, his accent adding a soothing touch to his words. "And my mother makes the best moussaka you'll ever taste."

Kulap smiled, seeking common ground in their shared love for food—the universal language that bridged their cultures.

"I can't wait to try it," she said.

In a quiet show of affection and support, Markos reached over and gave her hand a light squeeze. Kulap squeezed back, finding strength in their brief but significant contact. They could work through the difficulties of combining their worlds together.

After a brief moment of silence, Kulap couldn't resist asking, "Markos?"

He turned to her with a raised eyebrow. "Yes, my dear?" he replied in his smooth Greek accent.

"Is there anything I should remember or avoid doing? Like when you met my family... I had to explain the Wai greeting."

A smile tugged at the corners of Markos's mouth as he remembered the traditional Thai gesture—pressing one's palms together in a prayer-like position and bowing slightly. "Ah yes, that was a smart move," he said.

Kulap's heart quickened as she braced herself for what was to come. "What should I do to show respect?" she asked again.

Markos's tone became more serious as he answered, "You should know that my family can be quite intense." He chuckled nervously, but there was an underlying hint of unease in his eyes.

"They don't really understand personal space. They hug like they're trying to squeeze the life back into you, and they may ask personal questions that some find too invasive."

Kulap nodded, bracing herself for the embrace and the inquiries that would follow. Intimacy in Thailand required time and trust, and personal boundaries were highly prized. However, Markos and his family demonstrated intimacy through open communication and physical contact. She inhaled deeply, prepared to welcome this novel experience with an open mind and heart.

The expressway faded away behind them as they drove deeper into the heart of the city. The neighborhoods grew denser, the streets narrower, and the houses began to exude an old-world charm, each one holding untold stories of families much like the one Kulap was about to meet. Markos turned onto a familiar road, lined with elegant sycamore trees that whispered secrets in the wind—a path that led to a new beginning, an introduction, a fusion of Greek zest and Thai grace.

"Are you ready?" Markos asked softly, reaching out to touch her hand in reassurance.

"Ready as I'll ever be," she responded with a forced smile that belied her nerves.

They stepped out onto the cobblestone drive, and before they could even reach the carved front door, it swung open. A bunch of voices spilled out, a cacophony of Greek that swelled in the evening air. The first to emerge from the doorway was a robust woman with hair as dark as midnight and arms opened wide.

"Markos!" she bellowed, enveloping him in a fierce embrace that made Kulap half-expect to hear his ribs crack.

"Mom, this is Kulap," Markos managed to say once released from the bear hug.

"Ah, Kulap!" His mother suddenly hugged Kulap tightly, almost too tight to breathe. When she let go, Kulap noticed the comforting smell of oregano and lemon on her blouse. The warm scent helped her relax a little.

"Welcome, welcome!" his mother exclaimed, ushering them inside with enthusiastic gestures.

The living room was a mosaic of aunts and uncles, cousins of all ages, each more eager than the last to greet the newcomer. Questions flew faster than Kulap could process—about Thailand, her family, how she met Markos, and when they planned to marry. Each inquiry was punctuated by another warm hug or a pat on the back as if affirming their acceptance through touch.

Throughout the evening, Kulap felt the warmth radiating from Markos's family, an almost overwhelming heat that was equal parts intrusive and endearing. It was as if their love knew no bounds, and their curiosity had no filters. While it was at times too much, it was also somehow just right—their boisterous laughter echoing throughout the house and blending with the scents of baked lamb and cinnamon, creating a tapestry of new memories woven with threads of old traditions.

Sitting beside Markos at the crowded dining table, Kulap caught his eye and offered a small but knowing smile. His hand found hers under the tablecloth, giving it a reassuring squeeze. At that moment, amidst the loud stories and rapid-fire Greek, she realized that this was family—an acquired taste, perhaps, but one she was beginning to savor.

The hum of the car engine was a quiet lullaby compared to the symphony of farewells that had echoed through Markos's family home moments earlier. As they pulled away from the curb, the streetlamps of Toronto flickered over Kulap's face, revealing a mixture of relief and contemplation.

"Your family," she began softly, her voice a melodic contrast to the city's pulse, "they're like a... strong spice." She turned to look at him with dancing eyes, a mix of amusement and mild bewilderment evident in her expression. "An acquired taste."

As he tried to bridge the cultural divide between them, Markos laughed easily and reached across the center console for her hand.

"They can be overwhelming," he admitted with a nod, giving her hand a gentle squeeze. "But you handled it beautifully."

As she leaned back into her seat, the city skyline passed by in a blur of lights and shadows. She couldn't help but feel overwhelmed by the constant movement and energy of the city.

"It takes some getting used to," she said.

The night fell and the moon cast its soft glow over the bustling metropolis, Markos's phone buzzed on his nightstand. Groggily reaching for it, he checked the time before answering. "Hello, Mom," he said with a heavy sigh, his voice weighed down by sleepiness.

"Markos, agápi mou, did you get home safely?" His mother's voice was just as energetic as ever, undiminished by the late hour.

"Yes, we're home now. Everything's fine," he reassured her, sitting up slightly so as not to disturb Kulap, who slept peacefully beside him.

"Kulap is such a nice girl, very polite," his mother continued, her words laced with both affection and concern. "But she seems so shy, my boy. Did I scare her that much?"

Markos couldn't help but smile at the image of his mother furrowing her brow in worry. "She's just not used to our way yet, give her time."

"Of course, of course," his mother conceded with a loving sigh. "Στην οικογένεια, όλοι είναι σηⵗαντικοί, αλλά οι καινούργιοι πρέπει να βρουν τη θέση τους." she added in Greek - "In the family, everyone is important, but newcomers must find their place."

"Goodnight, my son. Take care of her," his mother said before sending him kisses over the phone.

"Goodnight," he replied, the line going dead as he placed the phone back onto the nightstand. He lay back down, watching Kulap's peaceful face lit by the moonlight. Yes, time was all they needed. With that thought *in mind, Markos closed his eyes and let the stillness of the night cradle them both in its comforting embrace.*

We are living dictionaries, our bodies' unvoiced language filled with untold truths that resonate louder than spoken words. In a world where first impressions are formed in fleeting moments—exactly seven seconds according to research (Van Edwards, 2024)—the quiet dance of our gestures, postures, and movements plays a crucial role in shaping perceptions. Recognizing the cultural variations of body language not only fine-tunes communication but also bridges divides across diverse societies.

Nalini Ambady's work shows how we can gather accurate insights into someone's character and behavior by merely observing their body language for a few seconds. This highlights the critical role non-verbal communication plays in human interactions (Ambady & Rosenthal, 1992). For example, sustained eye contact and open body language can earn you tags such as confident and approachable, as per an article published in International Journal of Academic Research in Business and Social Sciences. On the other hand, those who adopt closed or defensive postures often find themselves perceived as untrustworthy or disinterested (Jamri, Bakar, Wahab, Mahbob & Kahar, 2022).

In America, body language is easy to read because the culture is relaxed. Making eye contact shows honesty and confidence, and a firm handshake means respect and professionalism. An article in UT Permian Basin, contributes 55% of successful communication to non-verbal cues. However, it's vital to remember that extended eye contact can be seen as an aggressive challenge—thus highlighting the subtle balance in American non-verbal communication (UT Permian Basin).

Americans value personal space; conversations usually maintain about an arm's length distance. Nods and smiles are tools for friendly interaction, while open hands signal agreement and openness—highlighting individuality and directness, which pave the way for vibrant dialogues.

Canadian body language mirrors many American norms, but with added restraint—courtesy is key here. Canadians may lessen eye contact to avoid seeming invasive or overly assertive. Canadians engage less in physical expression than their American counterparts, often favoring subtle gestures and composed demeanor in social settings. Handshakes are softer yet equally common in formal settings—emphasizing professionalism without the intensity found in American greetings.

In addition, Canadians exhibit more restrained facial expressions, which is indicative of their culture's value of modesty and humility. This subtle use of body language promotes a respectful and thoughtful atmosphere (eDiplomat).

In Ghana, traditional customs and hierarchical respect significantly shape body language. Young people often exchange fist bumps as greetings; older individuals prefer handshakes enhanced with finger snapping—a unique blend of formality and local flair.

Eye contact is valued but must be balanced with deference when interacting with elders to avoid being seen as disrespectful, highlighting the role of cultural context in interpreting body language (Young, 2018).

Chinese body language subtly embodies cultural pillars such as hierarchy, modesty, and deference. Bowing slightly during formal greetings is a common practice China often use non-verbal communication to maintain harmony and avoid confrontation.

Minimal eye contact is typical; excessive directness can be seen as confrontational or disrespectful toward superiors. Gestures are often understated, emphasizing context and social relationships over individual expression (eDiplomat).

Hispanic cultures radiate warmth through their expressive body language—frequent hugs or cheek kisses coupled with engaging eye contact create a vibrant tapestry of non-verbal communication that beautifully complements verbal exchanges. Body language can convey affection and familiarity—playing a crucial role in trust-building. Understanding these norms is vital for successful interactions (Livermore, 2013).

The cultural tapestry of Europe is reflected in the wide variety of expressions seen in European body language. Northern European nations place a higher importance on formality and personal space, frequently keeping a greater physical distance when conversing, prioritizing verbal clarity and directness over bodily expression.

Conversely, Southern European countries lean towards more expressive non-verbal cues—frequent hand gestures and closer physical proximity during interactions. This divergence illustrates how cultural values shape body language—highlighting the importance of contextual understanding in cross-cultural communication.

Arabic-speaking cultures present a lively array of body language signals where firm handshakes, penetrating eye contact, and dynamic gestures play significant roles in communication. However, in more conservative environments, physical contact between genders is often avoided to uphold propriety — a testament to the intricacies of social engagements within varied cultural frameworks.

Moreover, the use of gestures in Arabic cultures tends to be more animated — individuals frequently use their hands for emphasis during dialogues. This vibrancy contributes to an inviting ambiance, underscoring the importance placed on personal relationships and communal ties (Zaharna, 1995).

Deciphering the mysteries of cultural subtleties in body language can be key to achieving effective communication and nurturing positive engagements. Each culture carries its distinct set of norms sculpted by historical, societal, and cultural forces. By approaching these disparities with finesse and sensitivity, we can master the art of cross-cultural exchanges, enriching both our personal and professional bonds.

Understanding body language requires more than just visual perception; it also requires cultural awareness and empathy. We must be mindful of the messages we convey through our postures and body language while interacting with people from different backgrounds. By doing this, we can promote a more welcoming and peaceful environment that honors the wide range of human expression.

Our bodies' silent language serves as a medium for communication that transcends geographical boundaries and cultural divides. By into the countless ways body language differs worldwide, we can nurture deeper connections and enhance our interactions with others. As we traverse an increasingly globalized world, embracing these cultural subtleties will augment our capacity for effective communication — laying down stepping stones toward greater understanding and collaboration.

Unforeseen Insights

As the golden sun began to set behind the buildings, casting a warm amber glow over Queen Alia International Airport, I leaned against the railing, my eyes scanning the bustling crowd of travelers spilling through the arrival gates. Each figure moved with a sense of purpose in their strides, weaving through the crowd like dancers in a choreographed performance.

And then, there she was - Youla. Her unmistakable auburn hair shone even from a distance as she made her way towards me, a heavy backpack slung over one shoulder. Her wide eyes flickered around, taking in the foreign sights and sounds of Amman before locking onto mine. A smile spread across her face, and she quickened her pace, gracefully navigating her way through the sea of people.

"Ahlan wa sahlan, Youla!" I greeted her in Arabic as she approached,

"Zdradsveh, Linoshka!" Youla replied with endearment, extending her hand for a shake - an etiquette she had diligently researched beforehand. But instead of shaking hands, I pulled her into a warm embrace and planted two kisses on her cheeks - one for hello and another for making the long journey from Minsk to be here.

"Wow," she gasped with slight breathlessness, her light blue eyes sparkling with surprise. "I did not expect such a greeting!"

"Welcome to Jordan," I laughed, linking my arm with hers. "Here, we are all about warmth. And you'll soon learn that our customs go beyond what's written in books."

Youla strolled the living room, admiring every inch of my family's house while her fingers tenderly traced the elaborate needlework on the cushion covers. Even the invitation card, which was embossed with intricate golden patterns, had piqued her interest when I first received it in the mail, demonstrating her seemingly limitless curiosity.

"An engagement party?" she asked, turning to me with a mixture of excitement and apprehension. "Here, in Amman?"

"Exactly," I replied, observing the joy in her eyes as she processed this idea. "It's for one of my cousins. His fiancée's family is from Syria."

Youla tilted her head, considering this information. "And we're going?"

"Of course we are," I said with a smile. "It wouldn't be the same without us. Plus, you'll get to meet relatives from Saudi Arabia and Palestine too. It's quite the occasion."

She nodded slowly, recognizing the significance of this social event. "So, what should I wear? Something modest, I presume?"

With its connotations of cultural barriers she was still attempting to cross, her inquiry hung in the air between us. I could picture her mentally going through her bag, which was full of well-chosen clothing that honored the traditions she had studied.

"Actually, Youla, you got to dress up," I instructed gently, noticing the flicker of surprise on her face. "Wear something elegant, something festive."

"Really?" she blinked in confusion. "But I thought - from all the articles I read - it suggested women should err on the side of conservative."

"Ah," I chuckled, understanding her hesitation. "Out in public, modesty is key. But among women, when it's just us celebrating, we embrace dressing up and feeling beautiful. You'll see."

"Intriguing," she said with a hesitant smile forming on her lips. "Every day here seems to unravel a new layer of what I thought I knew."

"Welcome again to Jordan," I teased playfully, nudging her arm. "Prepare to be dazzled."

Our laughter blended together in pure delight and anticipation for the evening ahead. We navigated through the crowded streets in our car, making our way to the engagement party. Youla sat beside me, her hands fidgeting with the fabric of her dress, a mixture of nerves and excitement radiating from her.

"Remember, we will be in a separate room for women," I reminded her, stealing a glance at her reflection in the car window. "And trust me, they will all be dressed to impress."

"Separate?" She turned to face me, curiosity evident in her wide eyes.

"Yes, it's like stepping into another world—one where colors and jewels are not only allowed but celebrated." I smiled, hoping to ease her into the vibrant contrast she was about to encounter.

As we entered the grand hall, the joyful sounds of music filled our ears, beckoning even the shyest guests to dance. The women's section was a sight to behold - a sea of elegance and style, each woman adorned in their finest attire. Youla's gaze darted around, taking in the sight of covered and uncovered women alike, each one more beautiful than the last. Her initial shock gave way to awe as she absorbed the vibrant atmosphere.

"Come, let's greet the bride-to-be," I said, guiding her through the crowd.

Every surface was adorned with fragrant jasmine, and the air was filled with the alluring scents of traditional foods. Plates brimming with mouthwatering treats that no visitor could resist were passed around insistently. In Jordan, being hospitable was an art form rather than merely a politeness.

"Try this," urged one of my aunts, placing a heaping serving of mansaf in front of Youla with a warm smile. "You must eat when you are our guest - it is how we show love."

Youla nodded gratefully, taking a bite and savoring the rich flavors. Her earlier reservations faded away as she began to enjoy the food and the company genuinely.

As the night progressed, Youla found herself surrounded by dancing women, their movements a celebration of joy and freedom within these walls. Their contagious laughter filled the room as they swayed to the music, and soon enough, Youla joined in with every step.

Another of my aunts told one of her old stories, and the group burst out laughing as she skillfully transitioned into another. Youla's sincere and unrestrained laugh blended in with the others.

"Did you hear the one about the camel and the merchant?" another aunt chimed in, her eyes twinkling mischievously. The women leaned in eagerly, anticipation hanging in the air like the lingering scent of incense.

With perfect comedic timing, she delivered the punchline, and once again, the room was filled with uproarious laughter.

As the evening drew to a close, the festivities toned down to peaceful conversations and warm smiles. I found Youla sitting on a luxurious brocade cushion, a content smile gracing her lips as she listened to a group of nieces sharing their own funny stories.

She turned to me, her eyes reflecting the soft glow of lanterns above us. "I never expected any of this," she confessed in awe. "In my previous perception, conservative culture meant that fun could not be openly expressed."

I understood her surprise; it was a common misconception. But tonight, Youla had experienced the heart of another tradition - resilient joy and the unbreakable bond of shared laughter.

Body language is a powerful way to communicate without words. However, what is polite in one culture might be rude in another. Understanding these differences helps avoid misunderstandings and improves communication. This topic looks at how certain gestures can be offensive in different cultures, using real examples and facts.

Distinct cultures possess their unique lexicon of body language cues that can vary dramatically in interpretation. Take, for instance, the thumbs-up sign, a universal symbol of approval in many Western nations like the United States and Canada. However, this same gesture can be viewed as crude or disrespectful in countries like Greece or parts of the Middle East.

Another instance is the "peace" sign usage. In America, flashing two fingers in a V shape with your palm facing outward typically signals peace or victory. But flip it around—the palm facing inward—in places like the UK, Australia or New Zealand, and you've just made an obscene gesture akin to flipping someone off. This illustrates how a simple twist can alter meaning entirely, emphasizing the critical role context plays in interpreting body language (Pease, 2008).

Certain physical cues also mirror deeper cultural sensitivities. In several Asian societies like Japan and China, there's an emphasis on maintaining composure and limiting overt gestures. Pointing at someone is generally deemed impolite; instead, people tend to use their entire hand to indicate towards someone else.

In many Indigenous cultures too, body language is imbued with profound meanings tied to respect and spirituality. In Native American communities, eye contact during a conversation can be interpreted differently based on the situation and relationship between the individuals. Some tribes might view prolonged eye contact as confrontational, while others see it as a sign of respect and attentiveness. This variability underscores the importance of understanding cultural backgrounds when interpreting body language.

The concept of personal space also plays a significant role in body language and varies considerably across cultures. For instance, in the United States and many Western societies, people usually maintain a distance of about 1.5 to 3 feet during conversations. However, in Latin American and Middle Eastern cultures, individuals often stand much closer—sometimes even touching during conversation. When someone from a culture that values distance interacts with someone from a touch-friendly culture, it could lead to feelings of unease or offense.

Hall's Proxemics theory outlines four distinct zones of personal space: intimate, personal, social, and public. Violating these zones can cause discomfort or misunderstanding—emphasizing the need for cultural consciousness in social interactions (Brown, 2001). For example, at a business meeting between Western and Middle Eastern professionals, one party may perceive the closer approach as friendly while the other sees it as an invasion of personal space.

Body language is an integral part of communication that varies widely across cultures. Gestures that are harmless or even positive in one culture can be offensive in another—highlighting the need for cultural sensitivity and awareness. By acknowledging and respecting these differences, we can foster more effective communication and avoid misunderstandings.

Navigating this intricate landscape requires openness and willingness to learn about different cultures non-verbal cues. As our world becomes increasingly interconnected understanding these intricacies can enhance both personal and professional relationships—contributing towards building a more harmonious global community.

Biking Encounter

Before taking a seat on the bench across from Fatima, Michael carefully parked his clean and shining bicycle against the brick wall that was warmed by the sun. The symphony of laughter and clinking silverware, as well as the sounds of noon conversation, filled the outdoor café, providing a peaceful setting for their meeting.

"Hey there, Fatima," he greeted her with a charming smile that gleamed as bright as the polished chrome on his bicycle. His rough and calloused hands, evidence of countless hours gripping handlebars, contrasted with the delicate way he handled the bread.

"How's your day going?"

Fatima, her dark eyes reflecting the calm waters of her hometown in Al-Mukalla, Yemen, nodded warmly at him.

"Good... and yours? I saw you racing down the street earlier; you looked like you were flying."

"Ah, nothing compares to the freedom of the road under your wheels," Michael replied, and he unwrapped his sandwich, his hands moving with precision as if they knew every gear and cable on his beloved bike.

"Any more crazy workouts or diets?" Fatima asked

"Not lately... but I got to keep in shape," he added between bites of his sandwich. "Coaching is more than just tactics and schedules. It's about fully immersing yourself in the ride, you know?" His gaze, so often scanning horizons and assessing terrains, met hers with an earnest intensity. Their conversation flowed effortlessly around them, similar to wheels turning on a familiar and well-traveled path.

"Ahh... how is the coaching going?" Fatima smiled, enjoying Michael's frequent funny stories

Leaning back against the warm bench, Michael momentarily forgot about his lunch as he watched a sparrow flit between tree branches overhead. He exhaled slowly, feeling the weight of his frustrations heavy on his shoulders.

"Actually," he began, pausing to find the right words, "I've been coaching a new group lately. They're women who have recently arrived from Afghanistan."

Fatima paused with her fork hovering mid-air, her salad forgotten as she regarded him with a curiosity that matched the attentive way he would watch his cyclists rounding a tight bend.

"That sounds like a great opportunity for them," she replied, encouraging him to continue.

"Yeah, you would think so," Michael grumbled, running a hand through his hair that bore faint lines from his helmet. "But it's been tough. Every time I try to offer advice or help them with their technique, they just... turn their backs on me. They don't even acknowledge my presence."

With a hint of pain and annoyance, the words came out. The tacit rejections he received from his players damaged his pride as a coach. He couldn't seem to get beyond this barrier, which tore at him like a never-ending anguish. It felt like a personal insult to the trust and camaraderie he tried to build each time one of them turned away without even responding.

He recounted an incident from that morning, his voice now laced with heat and exasperation. "I approached one of the girls to correct her posture, and she simply walked away. She didn't even give me a chance to explain why she must avoid injury."

Shaking his head in disbelief, Michael's thoughts mirrored the chaotic swirl of emotions within him. He had always viewed his role as a coach as clear-cut — to guide, to refine, to motivate. But these interactions, or lack thereof, left him feeling disrespected.

Fatima leaned forward with a gentle smile, her presence bringing a calming effect on the tension etched in Michael's brow. "Michael," she said softly, "you have to understand where these ladies are coming from." She paused thoughtfully, searching for the right words to bridge the cultural divide before them. "In Afghanistan, many women have had to see men as potential threats."

Her fingers plucked at her lunch absently as she continued, "It's not rudeness or arrogance you're witnessing. It's a protective shield they've been forced to build. They don't mean to disrespect you; they're simply acting on instinct, trying to safeguard themselves based on their upbringing."

Michael's eyes remained fixed on Fatima. The frustration that had been bubbling inside him began to dissipate, replaced by a newfound understanding. Setting his sandwich down slowly, he visibly relaxed as the weight of misunderstandings lifted from his shoulders.

"Ahh," he murmured, the word barely audible over the bustling sounds of the cafeteria. His gaze wandered past Fatima, focusing on a *distant point as her words sank in. It was like a light had been turned on, and suddenly, the room — once shrouded by his own preconceived notions — was now illuminated with a different perspective.*

"Fatima, that... changes everything." Michael's voice was low yet resolute, a newfound determination now taking root within him. He felt an unexpected kinship with his Afghan team members, a deep empathy for their guarded interactions. With this revelation, a new path opened up before him — one forged through a deeper understanding of their shared humanity.

Chapter Seven- Culture Part III: Unraveling the Norms

"When you travel, remember that a foreign country is not designed to make you comfortable. It is designed to make its own people comfortable."

— Clifton Fadiman

In the Shadows

Emily strode confidently across the plush carpet of the open-plan office, her heels clicking with purpose. Her sharp, tailored suit exuded authority and power as she made her way to Mark's desk. He was bent over a pile of papers and reports but straightened up immediately upon seeing her approach.

"Mark," Emily began without preamble, "have you had a chance to review Wei's latest report? It's exceptional, as always."

Mark nodded in agreement. "He has a knack for distilling complex data into digestible information. Plus, his recommendations save us a fortune in the long run."

"Exactly," Emily affirmed, tucking a loose strand of hair behind her ear. "His work is not only effective but also cost-conscious. He's an invaluable asset to our team."

Her brows furrowed slightly as she paused. It was an unusual hesitancy from someone who usually took decisive action. "But I'm hitting a roadblock trying to get him the recognition he deserves from upper management."

"Really?" Mark's voice was filled with surprise, "With the caliber of his work?"

"Unfortunately." Emily's frustration was evident in her tone. "It's like they can see the solutions but not the person behind them. No matter how

much I push for it, it doesn't seem to be enough to secure him the promotion he's earned."

Mark met her gaze, understanding the weight of what she was sharing. In their industry, talent like Wei's was game-changing, and both knew it deserved more than just quiet acknowledgment.

Emily leaned back against the cool glass walls of her office, crossing her arms as she considered Mark's puzzled expression. "It's like he doesn't register on their radar. They remember his solutions but struggle to recall his name in meetings."

Mark looked worried as he thought about what Emily said. He shifted his weight and straightened the papers on her desk without thinking. He wanted to show his need for order in the chaos of office life.

"Could it be a cultural difference?" he cautiously ventured, aware of the sensitivity of the topic. "Wei's background and approach might seem different to them. You know how these executives are, Emily. They tend to gravitate towards what is familiar and assertive, much like they see in themselves."

"Perhaps," Emily reluctantly conceded with a sigh, the thought resonating with her sense of fairness. "But it goes beyond that; it's also an issue of visibility. Wei's brilliance is quiet and meticulous — a stark contrast to the loud bravado that is celebrated in the boardroom."

"Exactly," Mark nodded, leaning forward slightly as if trying to grasp the solution from thin air physically. "In many Eastern cultures, there is a focus on collective achievement rather than individual recognition. Perhaps Wei's humility is being overshadowed by the other louder voices in the room."

Emily's expression softened as she acknowledged the truth in Mark's observation. Wei's modesty and dedication to team success over personal gain didn't align well with the company's culture of promoting individual achievements above all else.

Unseen yet ever-present, cultural norms are the invisible framework that molds our actions, the way we converse, and our interactions within our communities. To truly grasp these norms is akin to standing atop a mountain, surveying the vast landscape of human behavior in all its rich and varied forms. This includes how we perceive time, the ways we communicate, our balance between individuality and group identity, how power is distributed in society, the roles assigned to each gender, the rituals we hold dear, religious influences on daily life, societal manners, and etiquette, how conflicts are resolved and even our capacity to adapt to change. Each of these elements weaves together into an intricate tapestry of human connection that dictates how we understand and relate to one another across this diverse world.

The manner in which we communicate is a fundamental reflection of our cultural identity, shaping the way we interact with others and navigate social structures worldwide. The contrast between direct and indirect communication styles provides insight into how different cultures express ideas and emotions and manage disputes. Western societies like the United States, Germany, and the Netherlands often prize directness as it embodies transparency and honesty. This preference can streamline decision-making processes in professional settings by encouraging open expression of views without fear.

"Many English speakers in the United States hold the direct style as the most appropriate in most contexts. This is revealed in sayings like "don't beat about the bush", "get to the point", and "what exactly are you trying to say?" Although "white lies" may be permitted in some contexts, a direct style emphasizes honesty, openness, individualism, and forthrightness" (Rygg, 2012).

However, being very direct can sometimes create tension, especially in diverse workplaces. For example, an American boss giving honest feedback might seem rude or too harsh to employees from cultures that prefer indirect communication. This could lead to hurt feelings or a lack of motivation.

On the other hand, Asian countries like Japan, along with Latin American and some Middle Eastern nations, often lean towards subtle forms of communication where non-verbal cues and context are paramount. This is an indication of their cultural inclination towards subtlety over explicitness. Consequently, a Japanese worker might express disagreement through body language or vague wording rather than an outright denial.

"Courtesy often takes precedence over truthfulness, and this is consistent with the cultural emphasis on maintaining social harmony as the primary function of speech. This leads members of collectivistic cultures to give an agreeable and pleasant answer to questions when literal, factual answers might be unpleasant or embarrassing" (Rygg, 2012).

This reliance on contextual cues can complicate cross-cultural interactions. An American manager who values frankness may misconstrue a Japanese employee's hesitation as a lack of interest or commitment. In contrast, the Japanese worker might find the manager's straightforwardness aggressive, leading to potential miscommunication.

The cultural dimension spanning individualism and collectivism also plays a significant role in shaping social dynamics, including personal aspirations, work relationships, and community engagement.

"Collectivists are closely linked individuals who view themselves primarily as parts of a whole, be it a family, a network of co-workers, a tribe, or a nation. Such people are mainly motivated by the norms and duties imposed by the collective entity. Individualists are motivated by their own preferences, needs, and rights, giving priority to personal rather than to group goals" (Triandis, 1995).

Societies such as those in the United States, Canada, and many Western European countries prioritize personal success over communal achievements. This outlook fosters self-reliance, creativity, and personal expression but can also lead to feelings of isolation, especially among those who don't achieve the expected level of success. 95 (Livermore, 2013).

In contrast, collectivist cultures prevalent in many African, Asian, and Latin American countries prioritize group harmony and interdependence. Which leads to immigrants transitioning from collectivist societies to individualistic ones often reporting feelings of loneliness and disconnection as they adapt to a culture that celebrates individual achievements.

The concept of power distance, coined by Geert Hofstede, highlights how different cultures perceive and accept power disparities within social and organizational contexts. Cultures with high power distance, such as Malaysia, India, and many Arab nations, tend to respect hierarchical structures where questioning superiors is often frowned upon. This acceptance can foster stability within organizations but may also stifle creativity and perpetuate inequality (Hofstede, 1983).

Conversely, societies characterized by low power distance, like Sweden, New Zealand, and the Netherlands, advocate for equal interactions across all levels of hierarchy, fostering a collaborative work environment that encourages innovation.

Gender roles further complicate these dynamics, with cultural expectations often dictating responsibilities based on gender. Traditional gender roles remain prominent in many Middle Eastern cultures. In contrast, Scandinavian countries rank highest in gender equality, promoting women's active participation in the workforce, leading to a more inclusive society where diverse perspectives can flourish (Livermore, 2013).

Skyward Descent

Leaning back in her chair, Claire looked out the oval window to her left. She watched the Houston lights fade into darkness against the Texas night sky as the plane rose higher and higher. Her body was lulled into a state of serenity by the familiar sensations of the plane's engines. Even though it wasn't her first flight to São Paulo, something about this one felt different. She was traveling to see her Brazilian counterpart, Alejandro, whom she greatly respected for his careful planning and attention to detail.

As the cabin lights dimmed, Claire settled in for the long journey ahead. She couldn't help but wonder how their upcoming meeting would unfold. She smiled at the thought of Alejandro's amiable tardiness and his invitations for coffee, which always set the tone for their productive collaborations.

Claire opened her laptop and delved into the numbers and strategies that awaited her attention. But a gentle tap on her shoulder from an older businessman sitting beside her interrupted her focus. She turned to face him and offered a polite nod, to which he smiled.

"Work...work...work," he commented, glancing curiously at her device.

"Yes," Claire replied with a small smile. "There's always much to prepare before landing."

"Business never sleeps, I suppose," the man remarked with a chuckle, settling his hands comfortably on his lap.

"Indeed," Claire agreed, her fingers poised over the keyboard. "But sometimes, I can't help but wonder if we miss something in our haste." Her words hung in the air between them, revealing an internal debate she hadn't realized she was having.

"First time?" the man asked, breaking the steady hum of the aircraft with genuine curiosity.

Claire's hands paused their movement as she turned to face him fully. Her professional demeanor softened as she responded with a playful tone, "Actually, it's my third trip."

The man's smile widened, his eyes crinkling at the corners. "Oh? How do you like Brazil?"

"I absolutely adore it," Claire answered with genuine warmth. "The energy, the colors, everything about it is so vibrant and unique." She gestured with her hands, expressing her deep appreciation for the country's culture.

"But their sense of time...it can be a bit wonky," she confessed with a half-smile that didn't quite reach her eyes.

It was a subliminal nod to the internal clock she always carried with her, a steady metronome timed to the hectic pace of Houston's business community. Although she frequently found herself at odds with São Paulo's more flexible view of time, she was unable to resist the city's vibrant and energetic atmosphere. She couldn't help but feel a mixture of nostalgia and slight annoyance for this intriguing country she was going to land in once more as she sat back in her seat and looked out at the passing clouds.

His posture shifted ever so slightly, bringing him closer to her as if bridging the gap between their worlds. A gentle smile curved his lips, almost reverent in its softness, as if he were about to impart a secret long known to those who had tread a path similar to his own. The hum of the aircraft's engines provided a soothing backdrop for his voice, a soothing timbre that seemed oddly comforting against the artificial noise.

"It isn't a disregard for time," he said, words flowing like honey from his lips. "Rather, it's an appreciation — a recognition, really — that moments spent nurturing relationships are invaluable."

The weight of his words hung in the air, causing ripples in Claire's carefully constructed worldview. She paused, her fingers resting idly on her laptop's keyboard. The screen glowed with the half-finished *presentation she had been perfecting, yet it now seemed to fade from her focus.*

As she gazed out the window at the passing clouds and landscape below, thoughts and memories flooded her mind. For the first time in what felt like forever, she found herself reflecting on her own hurried lifestyle back home. Her days were a blur of meetings, emails, and deadlines – a ceaseless pursuit of efficiency where its brevity and tangible outcomes measured each interaction. She realized, with a start, how often she rushed through conversations without truly engaging, her mind always ticking ahead to the next task or goal.

The old man's eyes crinkled with a knowing twinkle as he delivered his parting shot, a subtle wink accentuating the weight of his words. "You'll find," he said, his voice low and infused with a lifetime of experience, "that the most important meetings happen not in boardrooms but over coffee, where the gift of time and connection takes center stage."

As she watched the ever-changing landscape pass by below, Claire felt a sense of calm and clarity wash over her. Her thoughts, no longer compartmentalized into neat segments of time and productivity, now flowed together with a newfound fluidity. She understood the value of taking the time to truly connect with others, to savor each moment instead of rushing through them. As she closed her laptop and settled back into her seat, she made a mental note to slow down and appreciate the present more often.

The social fabric of any society is deeply woven with cultural norms that shape the way individuals behave, communicate, and form relationships. A key aspect of these norms is how societies perceive time, which can be broken down into past, present, or future-oriented perspectives. Understanding these perceptions is a crucial step in appreciating how different cultures interact and navigate their societal landscapes.

Cultures steeped in past orientation, such as those prevalent in many Asian countries like China and Japan, place considerable emphasis on tradition, history, and collective memory. In these societies, decision-making often mirrors an understanding of historical contexts and values passed down by ancestors. For instance, in Japan, practices like "Hinomaru" (the national flag) and "Kintsugi" (the art of repairing pottery with gold) underscore a deep respect for historical continuity and the beauty found in imperfection (Livermore, 2013).

In India, this focus on the past is evident in the family structure, where lineage and heritage significantly influence life choices. The decision-making process here often prioritizes long-term communal welfare over individual aspirations. Arranged marriages in India are an example of this mindset, where extensive discussions about family backgrounds are common.

Some cultures focus on the present and enjoying life in the moment. Many Indigenous cultures celebrate changes in the seasons and nature's cycles. This way of thinking helps people appreciate life as it happens and value strong community connections more than long-term planning.

In Latin American cultures, the concept of "mañana" (tomorrow) reflects a relaxed attitude towards time, emphasizing flexibility over punctuality, which can strengthen community bonds but may also lead to challenges when deadlines need to be met (Livermore, 2013).

Future-oriented cultures like those found in America or Germany prioritize planning ahead along with setting and achieving goals. This belief is reflected in the American emphasis on "the American Dream," which encourages individuals to strive for personal and professional advancement through hard work, being a high-achiever means being punctual (Heffernan, 2014).

In Germany, the concept of "ordnung" (order) permeates societal values, leading to highly structured environments where punctuality and meticulous planning are expected. The precision Germans are known for in engineering, and technology reflects a future-oriented mindset that values foresight and reliability (Baur, 2020).

Cultural rituals often embody societal values reflecting the dominant time orientation of a culture. These rituals strengthen community bonds offering a sense of belonging. For instance, Diwali in India symbolizes the victory of light over darkness and is steeped in historical significance. Thanksgiving in America emphasizes gratitude and family unity, showcasing a blend of present and future orientations as families gather to reflect on their blessings while planning ahead.

Religious beliefs also shape moral values, often intertwining with a culture's time orientation. In countries like Saudi Arabia, Islamic principles govern various aspects of daily life, including dress codes, behavior, and social interactions aligning with a collectivist past-oriented mindset (Livermore, 2013).

In contrast, secular societies like those found in many European countries often exhibit more relaxed social norms regarding personal expression, allowing for individual achievement and fostering environments that encourage innovation.

Social etiquette is key when navigating interpersonal interactions across different cultural contexts, with customs related to greetings, dining practices, and gift-giving varying significantly based on cultural norms.

In Japan, bowing signifies respect, acknowledging hierarchical relationships reflecting tradition, whereas Western cultures prefer firm handshakes, symbolizing confidence aligning with their future-oriented mindset.

Dining practices vary widely, too; Middle Eastern cultures emphasize hospitality through communal meals reflecting a present-oriented focus. Western dining often emphasizes individual portions, prioritizing efficiency and aligning with future-oriented values.

Gift-giving customs illustrate cultural nuances; collectivist cultures view gifts as symbols of relationship strength given during significant events, while individualistic cultures may view gift-giving as transactional, focusing on individual achievements.

Peeling back the layers of cultural norms exposes a complex web where time orientation subtly shapes behavior, communication patterns, and societal dynamics. By probing into aspects like past reverence or future focus, cultural rituals, religious impacts on society, accepted etiquette, conflict resolution tactics, and cultural flexibility – we unlock deeper understandings of human interplay.

Successfully traversing these diverse cultural terrains demands empathy, awareness, and an open heart toward diversity. As globalization continues weaving societies closer together like threads on a loom, grasping these cultural norms becomes imperative for nurturing effective communication and fostering harmonious relationships. By truly valuing these intricate norms that make up different cultures around us - we can better steer through the hurdles presented by our increasingly interconnected globe - enhancing our collective capacity to work together and flourish amid diversity.

Finding Home in Unexpected Places

Nestled in the vibrant city of The Hague, I discovered an unexpected friendship with a Lebanese man named Samer. From our first conversation, his stories of Lebanon's rich history and warm culture captivated me. When he offered an invitation to visit, I eagerly accepted.

My journey to Lebanon was nothing short of enchanting. As I stepped onto the bustling streets of Beirut, often referred to as the "Paris of the Middle East," I was immediately struck by the harmonious blend of old and new architecture. The air was thick with the scent of spices and freshly baked bread from the lively markets, where Lebanese women glided through in their stylish attire, turning heads with every step. The energy was palpable, and I felt a sense of belonging.

The highlights of my trip were unforgettable. History whispered through the ruins of Baalbek, while the serene views along the waterfront at Byblos provided a peaceful place for reflection. Similar to my experiences in Nigeria, I noticed how much Lebanese people value celebrating life and creating a party atmosphere wherever they go.

One sunny afternoon, Samer invited us to his family's village, hidden in the mountains. As we wound through the scenic roads, excitement bubbled within me. Upon arrival, we were welcomed by Samer's family as if we were long-lost friends. Their hospitality knew no bounds; plates overflowing with delicious food were presented before us, and laughter filled the air. It felt like we were embraced not just by one family but by an entire community.

Samer casually brought up a party at a friend's house three mountains away during our visit. I found the idea of measuring distances in the mountains to be both exciting and alien. Our party chose to participate in the celebration without official invitations. I was astonished to see that we were welcomed with open arms as we laughed and danced with new acquaintances; music pulsated through the air.

As night fell and the mountains were bathed in a golden glow, I found myself swept up in the rhythm of the festivities. Samer and his friends gathered us around to teach us the dabke, a traditional Lebanese folk dance. With each stomp and clap, the joyous energy of the music resonated within me. Dancing the dabke was more than just a cultural experience; it was a way to connect, share in the moment's happiness, and embrace Lebanese hospitality.

Reflecting on this experience, I couldn't help but notice the similarities with gatherings in my home country of Nigeria, where parties *are always overflowing with guests, and relationships hold more importance than formalities. In both cultures, hospitality is a cornerstone, and being surrounded by people eager to share their joy made me feel at home.*

As the sun set behind the mountains, casting a warm glow over our celebration, I realized that my journey in Lebanon was not just a visit; it was a reminder of the universal bonds that unite us all. Through immigrating and experiencing different cultures, I learned that at our core, we are not so different. We all long for connection, love, and a sense of belonging. The laughter shared, the meals enjoyed, and the friendships formed transcended borders, showing that beneath our diverse backgrounds and traditions lies a shared humanity—a profound truth that continues to shape my understanding of the world.

Chapter Eight- The Authority Effect

"Authority without wisdom is like a heavy axe without an edge--fitter to bruise than polish."

— Anne Bradstreet

Graduation Under the Jordanian Sun

I plucked up the confidence to go up to my father as the sun began to set, bathing the Amman sky in a warm glow. He was sitting in his favorite armchair, encircled like a fortress by tall piles of books and newspapers. He had an air of intelligence and wisdom that he so desperately wanted me to imitate, and his glasses rested on the bridge of his nose.

"Baba," I began, my voice barely above a whisper in the peaceful evening ambiance, "I've been thinking..."

He looked up at me, a silent prompt to continue.

"Maybe I could take a year off before university? To...to figure out what I really want to study."

The air seemed to still be around us, the weight of my words hanging in the air like a delicate chandelier swaying precariously after a sudden gust.

My parents came from different backgrounds—Jordanian traditions and Russian strength—and they strongly believed in the importance of education. Our home was filled with diplomas hanging on the walls like family pictures, silently reminding me that skipping university was unthinkable. My father often spoke passionately about the value of a professional degree, just as eagerly as he discussed politics or the perfect way to make Turkish coffee.

"Education is your foundation, Lina," he would say, his dark eyes shining with conviction. "Build it strong."

My mother, with her stories of snowy Russian winters and the warmth of literature, would nod in agreement, her own academic achievements a testament to the merging of two worlds and ideologies.

My father set aside his newspaper with deliberate precision, but the tense tightening of his jaw betrayed his true feelings. "Lina," he said calmly but with an underlying tone of steel, "there is nothing to think about. Your options are clear - engineer, doctor, or lawyer."

His words sliced through my hopeful thoughts like a sharp blade, shutting doors to unexplored rooms that I wasn't even allowed to glance into. The path ahead of me was well-worn and predictable—a net woven from threads of safety and expectation.

Summoning all of my courage, I dared to continue the conversation. "What about literature or history?" My words were careful and hopeful, pushing against the boundaries of my father's expectations.

"Literature? History?" He repeated my words as if they were foreign concepts, his brows knitting together in disbelief. "And what are you going to do with that degree, Lina? You will never make enough money to support yourself." His voice was not unkind, but it carried the weight of finality—an unspoken decree that such paths were frivolous for someone like me.

The defeat was palpable, seeping into my pores and settling heavily in my chest. The dreams I harbored, filled with the romance of bygone eras and the beauty of prose, seemed to crumble with each word he spoke. I watched them scatter like dust motes dancing lazily in the slanting sunlight through our living room window.

"Lina ... I love you, and I want what is best for you ... in this world of ours. I want to make sure you always have choices in life, and those choices come at a cost; you need a professional degree."

I nodded, but he continued, "The world can say whatever it wants, in the end, those who bring bread home make the decision ... these are not unkind words; these are facts of life," he stated, then looked at me kindly.

"As you grow and start your own life, I want to be at peace that you have the tools to make your choices, Lina ... not be bound by financial dependencies on anyone."

In the end, I nodded, a silent surrender to the invisible forces that had stealthily dictated every milestone of my life. I turned away from him, retreating to the sanctuary of my room where university brochures lay scattered across my bed like fallen soldiers on a battlefield of my future.

With a sigh that felt like it carried the weight of all my unspoken dreams, I picked up a pen and filled out the application forms. My rebellion, small and quiet, took shape in the box I checked—Chemical Engineering. Not the mechanical or electrical disciplines my father held in high regard, but my own subtle act of defiance. It was a choice that still paid homage to his vision yet allowed me a semblance of agency—a whisper of me within the narrative he authored.

In the vast, interconnected landscape of our modern world, it's crucial to grasp the subtle differences in how cultures interpret titles, levels of education, positions, and authority. These factors mold social interactions, shape professional relationships, and influence personal identities.

Titles act as badges of status, expertise, and authority across various cultures. They don't just showcase an individual's accomplishments but also set the tone for social interactions and relationships. For instance, in East Asian societies like Japan and China, titles are key indicators of social hierarchy and respect. They're deeply embedded in cultural practices, especially in professional settings. In Japan, the "senpai-kohai" (senior-junior relationship) concept is central to their culture. Titles are used to recognize seniority and experience, with younger individuals often addressing their seniors by their titles, such as "sensei" for teachers or "shachō" for company presidents (Japan Dev Team, 2024).

Similarly, in China, titles denote professional rank and educational qualifications. The usage of "Doctor" or "Professor" is common in academic and medical contexts, reflecting the significance placed on educational attainment.

On the other hand, Western cultures like America and Canada lean towards a more egalitarian approach where people prefer being addressed by their first names promoting informality and approachability. However, in formal business settings, titles still hold considerable weight, particularly for high-ranking positions.

Education levels have a profound influence on social mobility and personal identity across cultures. The importance placed on education varies significantly, shaping career opportunities and societal perceptions. In Nordic countries like Sweden and Finland, education is highly valued and considered a fundamental right. These nations emphasize equality and accessibility in education, resulting in high educational attainment levels. For example, over 60% of the Swedish population holds a tertiary education degree contributing to a culture that prioritizes meritocracy (Trading economics, 2025).

However, in many developing countries, access to education can be limited, with educational attainment not always correlating with professional opportunities. In India, for instance, while over 10% of the population holds a degree, disparities persist in educational access, particularly in rural areas (Waghmare, 2024).

Job roles reflect social status and influence interpersonal dynamics across cultures. The importance assigned to job positions varies, shaping societal norms and expectations. In many Middle Eastern cultures like Saudi Arabia, job roles are closely tied to social status and familial expectations, whereas high-ranking positions in government or business are associated with prestige and honor.

In Latin America, personal relationships play a crucial role in professional interactions, with the concept of "personalismo" emphasizing the importance of interpersonal connections in career advancement. For instance, in Brazil, while job titles may carry significant prestige, the relational aspect of work is equally important, with individuals often relying on personal networks to secure job opportunities, making informal interactions as vital as formal qualifications (Conde-Brooks, 2023).

Visitors from Germany

Jason tapped his fingers on the frost-kissed windowpane of 'Leaves & Beans,' a cozy café nestled in the heart of Ottawa, watching the world hustle by in a blur of winter coats and scarves. Inside, the warmth was a welcome reprieve, carrying with it the rich aroma of ground coffee beans and freshly baked pastries.

"Hey, Jason!" A familiar voice cut through the hum of quiet conversations and the clinking of porcelain.

He turned and saw Carlos moving between the tables, smiling widely. Carlos had his arm linked with Clara's, who looked effortlessly graceful, even bundled up against the cold Canadian weather. Her golden hair shone in the light, making her look like someone from a fairy tale.

"Carlos! Clara!" Jason rose from his seat, the wooden chair scraping slightly against the tiled floor. He embraced his friends, feeling the residual cold from their clothes seep into his warm sweater. "I almost didn't recognize you two under all those layers," he chuckled, eyeing the heavy coats and scarves they had yet to shed.

"Ah, this Canadian winter is something else," Carlos said, his accent now carrying a twinge of German cadence that hadn't been there during their university days.

"Freiburg may get cold, but it's nothing compared to this," Clara added, her eyes twinkling as she unwound her scarf, revealing a delicate

necklace underneath. She seemed to carry an air of the old-world charm, a stark contrast to the modern bustle outside.

"Come on, let's sit down. You must be freezing," Jason said, motioning towards the window booth he'd snagged.

As they settled into their seats, the waitress came over with a knowing smile; Jason was a regular here. "The usual, Jason?"

"Make it three," he replied, nodding toward his friends. "They're visiting from Germany for a month."

"Ah, Willkommen!" The waitress smiled at Carlos and Clara before bustling off to prepare their drinks.

"Thanks, man," Carlos said, easing into the conversation as they removed their outerwear. "It's great to be back, if only for a little while."

"Definitely," Jason agreed, leaning back in his seat, feeling the familiarity and nostalgia wash over him. It was like no time had passed since their carefree university days, despite the oceans and years that now lay between them.

A warm, enticing aroma filled the air as steam rose from the coffee mugs that were placed in front of them. Jason observed Clara leaning back in her chair and her eyes darting about the cafe's comfortable atmosphere while Carlos gripped his mug with both hands as though attempting to absorb its warmth.

"So, how's life in Freiburg?" Jason asked, breaking the comfortable silence. "Must be quite a change from Canada, huh?"

Carlos set his mug down with a clink, a wry smile forming on his lips. "You have no idea. Everything is different—the language, the culture, the bureaucracy..."

"Ah, the famous German efficiency," Jason joked but noticed Carlos's expression was less amused than he'd expected.

"Efficiency is one word for it," Carlos said with a chuckle that didn't quite reach his eyes. "When I first moved there, I tried to get a credit card. Thought it would be a simple process—walk in, show my Canadian credit history, walk out with a card."

"And...?" prompted Jason when Carlos paused, a furrow forming between his brows.

"Turns out, my Canadian credit history might as well have been written in crayon for all the good it did." Carlos shook his head, a look of frustration flashing across his features. "They wouldn't accept it. Insisted I had no financial background they could trust. I even showed them my savings—cold, hard cash—but that didn't work either."

"Really?" Jason leaned forward, intrigued by the complexity of something he'd taken for granted back home. "So, what did you do?"

Carlos sipped his espresso, the bitter taste mingling with the sweetness of nostalgia as he turned to Clara. Her eyes, clear and intelligent, held a hint of laughter as they shared an unspoken memory. She gave a small nod as if permitting him to tell their tale.

"It was Clara, actually," Carlos began, his voice warm with gratitude. "She worked at the bank where I was trying to get my credit card. After watching me hit wall after wall, she approached me."

Clara interjected, her accent coloring the words charmingly, "He was so persistent, yet so utterly baffled by our system. It was endearing and, quite frankly, exasperating to witness."

Jason leaned in closer, captivated.

"Clara told me something was missing in my application—a detail that seemed trivial to me but crucial in Germany," Carlos continued.

With a playful glint in her eye, Clara recounted the advice she had given him. "I simply said, 'Add your academic title—Dr. Carlos—and watch what happens.'"

The skepticism Carlos had felt then seemed to resurface momentarily on his features. "I couldn't believe it would make a difference. In Canada, titles are not flashed around like that—not for credit cards."

"Ah, but in Germany, respect for titles is ingrained in our culture. It's a key to many doors," Clara explained, her lips curving into a knowing smile.

Shaking his head in disbelief, Carlos finished their story. "So, I took her advice, skeptically adding those two little letters—Dr.—before my name. And would you believe it? Within three days, I had my credit card."

Jason whistled softly, shaking his head at the thought. "Just like that?"

"Just like that," Carlos confirmed, his gaze fond as he looked at Clara. "And it was all thanks to her."

Carlos leaned back in the chair, a hint of triumph playing on his lips as he recounted another tale from his European venture. "The credit card was just the beginning. When it came to securing a lease for an apartment, I hit another wall."

"Let me guess," Jason interjected, a wry smile pulling at the corners of his mouth, "you whipped out the 'Dr.' title again?"

"Exactly!" Carlos's voice was tinged with both amusement and exasperation. "I filled out application after application, but nothing stuck. Then, remembering what Clara had taught me, I prefaced my name with 'Dr.' on the next one."

"And just like that, you got the place?" Jason asked, eyebrows raised in mild disbelief.

"A few days later, the landlord was handing me the keys," Carlos replied, spreading his hands in a gesture of easy success.

Jason furrowed his brow, the confusion evident in his eyes as he tried to reconcile this foreign concept with his Canadian sensibilities. "But why *does a title sway so much weight? Isn't it about proving you can pay the rent?"*

"Titles carry a different kind of currency there," Clara chimed in, her voice smooth and assured. "It's not just about financial means; it's about status, reliability. If you're a doctor or professor, it implies a level of responsibility and trust."

"Here, it's your credit score and pay stubs that open doors," Jason mused, still grappling with the idea. "There, a couple of letters before your name can unlock them."

"Culture is curious, isn't it?" Carlos said, raising his cup in a mock toast. "Sometimes it's not the numbers in your bank account, but the letters in front of your name that make all the difference."

Different cultures interact with law enforcement and the justice system in unique ways, influenced by history, society, and politics. The way people see, follow, and enforce laws can vary greatly between cultures. To build peaceful and inclusive societies, it's important to understand these differences. This discussion looks at how law enforcement is viewed in Africa, Asia, Europe, and the Americas.

In some places, such as the Scandinavian countries of Sweden and Norway, police authority enjoys a high level of public trust. This faith stems from robust social welfare systems, minimal corruption levels, and strong public accountability measures. Transparent policing practices coupled with initiatives like community meetings where citizens can air their grievances contribute to this trust.

"In 2022, trust in the police was highest in the Netherlands (58%) and Denmark (58%)" (Brown, 2023).

Sweden's approach to policing is built around community engagement – officers are often seen more as community members than enforcers of law. Emphasizing preventive measures over punitive actions has led to lower crime rates, which further reinforces public confidence in the force (Hallman Jecic, 2020).

Norway, too, shares a similar philosophy when it comes to policing - focusing on de-escalation and rehabilitation rather than punishment (Akkoyun, 2024). The emphasis on communication and negotiation during conflict resolution has led to a steady drop in violent crime rates, according to Norwegian Police Directorate data (Statics Norway).

On the other side of the spectrum lie countries where authoritarian governance or systemic corruption has eroded public trust in law enforcement agencies. Citizens here view police as instruments of state power rather than protectors of public safety.

Mexico serves as an apt example where widespread corruption has bred deep-seated distrust in police authority among its populace.

People are unsure about efforts to change the police force. Because many don't trust law enforcement, communities have started their own safety programs. In places like Mexico City, neighborhoods have set up watch groups and ways to solve conflicts on their own.

Brazil, too, grapples with a pronounced distrust in police, especially within marginalized communities. A report by the Brazilian Forum on Public Safety states that over 6,000 people were killed by police in 2020, disproportionately impacting Black and low-income individuals. This has fostered a culture of fear and resentment towards the police, particularly in favelas (informal settlements) (Brazil 2022 Human Rights Report).

The idea of 'community policing' has been introduced in some Brazilian cities but faces resistance due to historical grievances and ongoing violence. Many residents feel that police presence only escalates tensions rather than providing safety. This leads to alternative forms of community organization where local leaders work to establish security without involving the police.

In Africa, interactions with law enforcement are colored by colonial histories, societal norms, and political realities. Many African countries face issues related to corruption, limited resources, and historical grievances that shape public perceptions of the police (Gashaw, 2017).

South Africa's apartheid legacy continues to influence community-police relationships. Despite efforts by the post-apartheid government towards reforming the police force, mistrust remains high among Black communities who bore the brunt of systemic discrimination.

"In 2022, trust in the police was lowest in Mexico (13%) and South Africa (16%)" (Brown, 2023).

This mistrust often leads to tensions, particularly in informal settlements where any display of police authority is met with hostility. Instances of police brutality further compound these tensions, leading to the emergence of community organizations advocating for accountability and transparency within law enforcement practices.

Nigeria, too, presents significant challenges when it comes to law enforcement authority. The Special Anti-Robbery Squad (SARS), a unit under the Nigerian Police Force, has faced widespread criticism for human rights abuses, including extrajudicial killings and extortion. The #EndSARS movement, which gained international attention in 2020, spotlighted the urgent need for police reform and the power of social media as a tool for demanding accountability (Humans Rights Watch, 2021).

In Kenya, public trust in police is similarly low due primarily to corruption and allegations of human rights violations. While community policing initiatives have been introduced to bridge the gap between law enforcement and communities, their effectiveness is often stymied by a pervasive culture of impunity.

"Kenyans' trust in police is, consequently, staggeringly low: five surveys over the time period 2011–2022 show that more than 60% of the population report no or just a little trust in the police" (Mutahi , Höglund & Elfversson, 2024).

Grassroots organizations in Kenya are working towards enhancing community engagement with law enforcement, emphasizing transparency and accountability. Programs fostering dialogue between police and community members aim to build trust and improve public safety.

Interactions between law enforcement agencies and Indigenous communities in countries like Canada and Australia can be particularly strained. Indigenous peoples often have their own legal traditions, which may not align with colonial legal structures.

In Canada, the Royal Canadian Mounted Police (RCMP) have faced criticism for how they interact with Indigenous communities. This has led to a movement calling for more respect for Indigenous rights and independence. The Assembly of First Nations has shared many reports showing the need for police to understand and respect Indigenous traditions and laws. Some programs that involve the community and use Indigenous practices have helped build trust and improve relationships (AFN release, 2024).

In Japan, police officers are generally held in high regard, with a potent cultural focus on maintaining societal harmony. The notion of "shame" holds significant sway in Japanese society, often acting as a deterrent against law-breaking through fear of social exclusion rather than legal penalties. This unique cultural viewpoint contributes to Japan's remarkably low crime rates, as societal pressure nudges individuals towards adherence to the law (Tran, 2017).

However, this doesn't mean it's without its own set of challenges. Instances of over-policing can surface, particularly when dealing with minority communities like the Burakumin. Despite an overall low crime rate, there have been situations where policing practices disproportionately zero in on marginalized groups, leading to debates about the fair application of the law.

Interactions between culture and law enforcement are intricate tapestries woven from historical contexts, societal values, and community trust. In cultures characterized by high levels of trust in their police forces, such as Sweden and Norway, cooperation and preventive strategies bolster public safety while encouraging community involvement. On the other hand, countries like Mexico, Brazil, South Africa, and Nigeria grapple with pervasive distrust, which can prompt alternative forms of community organization and conflict resolution.

Police Siren

The sound of my children's joyous laughter mingled with the cheerful chirping of birds in the spring air. The suburban street of Vancouver, British Colombia, was our playground, lined with modest homes whose front lawns were beginning to burst with vibrant blooms. As we played tag on the sidewalk, our footsteps created a playful rhythm that echoed through the neighborhood.

"Tag! You're it, Daddy!" Faramade shouted, her eyes sparkling with mischief. At barely six years old, she already had a mischievous streak and loved teasing me during our games.

"You'll never catch me!" I exclaimed, pretending to stumble as I scooped up my little boy, Adeyemi, in my arms. We spun around until everything became a blur of color and laughter. Adeyemi's delighted squeals filled the air as he clung tightly to my strong arms.

Suddenly, the whoosh of an approaching vehicle cut through our joyful bubble. I turned just in time to see a black and white cruiser roll past, its familiar insignia standing out against the blue sky.

"Police car, police car!" Faramade chanted with childlike fascination, pointing excitedly at the passing vehicle.

"Cool!" Adeyemi echoed, tracing the car's path with his tiny finger.

But as the cruiser disappeared around the corner, a heavy silence settled over me. The sound of my children's innocent admiration was drowned out by the pounding of my heart, which now matched the distant echo of a siren - one that wasn't even there. My smile faded, and my muscles tensed as memories flooded my mind, transporting me across continents and years.

I was no longer in Vancouver's secure streets. Rather, I found myself driving a car with red and blue lights flashing in my rearview mirror as I was taken back to Lagos, Nigeria. My palms began to perspire in the Nigerian heat as the siren's shriek cut through the car's soft hum.

"Stay calm," I murmured to my girlfriend beside me, her eyes reflecting a familiar fear. We watched as the police car idled behind us for a moment too long, an unsettling stillness before the doors swung open.

Two officers emerged, their crisp uniforms standing out against the chaotic backdrop of Lagos's streets. They sauntered towards our car, their mirrored sunglasses reflecting a distorted version of the world they patrolled. The taller officer's confident demeanor and tap on the window sent a shiver down my spine.

"Good afternoon, officer," I said politely as I rolled down the window, determined to remain courteous despite my growing unease.

"I.D.," the officer demanded without preamble, his gaze already scanning beyond my offered driver's license into the intimate space of our vehicle. He scrutinized every corner as if expecting to find contraband or a hidden criminal.

"Where are you coming from?" The second officer leaned in closer, his breath carrying the spicy scent of chewed kola nut. His calculating eyes scanned our car and took inventory.

"Just visiting family," I responded, trying to keep my voice steady and hide my racing heart. My girlfriend sat silently next to me; her hands folded tightly in her lap - a picture of contained anxiety.

"Going anywhere special?" the first officer continued with an undercurrent of threat woven through his casual tone. Even though we were innocent and had nothing to hide, their presence alone was enough to make us feel vulnerable and on edge.

"I'm just on my way home," I replied, trying to keep my tone even and my nerves from showing. I met the steely gazes of the officers, staring back at me with a coldness that sent shivers down my spine.

"Step out of the car," the taller officer commanded, his voice brooking no argument. The doors creaked open reluctantly, like a warning of the unfortunate fate awaiting us. As we emerged, I noticed a flicker of satisfaction in the officer's eyes - a predator reveling in the moment before the pounce.

"I no trust this man," muttered the second officer in broken English with feigned concern while rifling through my glove compartment without any regard for privacy. "We need to take you in for further questioning."

My protests died on my lips, leaving a bitter taste of powerlessness and dust from passing cars. My girlfriend was ordered into the back of the police van whilst the tall officer sat in the front seat of my car as I followed his directions to the police station. The ride to the station was a blur, each bump on the road jolting me back to reality - a reminder of where we were and what we were facing.

When we arrived, the fluorescent lights of the station hummed with apathetic sterility, casting an unsettling brightness over the stark holding area. We were ushered behind the police counter, the panel separating the counter from the throws of freedom closing behind us with a final thud that seemed to seal our fate.

As hours passed by slowly, time ticking away on the clock above the door, my thoughts turned to my mother. And like clockwork, she appeared at the threshold of our makeshift holding area - her presence commanding attention despite her small stature.

"Mom," I breathed out in relief, but shame still weighed heavy on my chest.

"Hush now," she silenced me with a look that spoke volumes without words. She turned to the officers and began negotiating our release with a calm determination only a mother who knows her child is innocent would do. I watched as money changed hands - an all too familiar exchange in a world where justice had its own price.

We left the station with the weight of that exchange heavy on our shoulders. It was a dance my mother and I had mastered, learned in a world where survival required constant payment. And even though I was now thousands of miles away from those streets, the impact of those moments still lingered - an indelible mark on my soul.

As my son's small hand gripped mine, his palm felt clammy, reminding me of how close we had come to losing everything. For a moment, I stood frozen, grappling with the ghosts of a life I had left behind—one where the sight of a police car evoked fear and danger instead of safety.

But then, I forced a smile on my face and crouched down to meet my children's curious eyes. "Yes, it's a police car," I said, trying to keep my voice steady despite the turmoil inside. "It keeps us safe here, okay?"

"Okay, Daddy!" Faramade chirped happily, already moving on and pulling at my hand to continue our game. Adeyemi nodded solemnly, his young mind still processing the shiny vehicle that had momentarily captured his imagination.

"Let's go," I said as I stood back up, feeling like a protective father once again as I led my family away from the haunting memories and towards the warmth of our home.

Chapter Nine- Out of Place, Yet at Home

"The ache for home lives in all of us, the safe place where we can go as we are and not be questioned."

– Maya Angelou

A Piece of Punjab in Toronto

Sukhdeep's fingers danced delicately over the globe, tracing the long journey from Punjab to Toronto. The continents were mere specks beneath his touch. Still, the significance of their upcoming relocation was palpable in the tension of his body and the bright anticipation shining in his eyes. This move promised a new life filled with opportunities and dreams waiting to be realized. As his fingers lingered on Canada, Sukhdeep couldn't help but feel a sense of pride at the golden emblem of the corporation that had offered him a position, a symbol of his hard work and dedication.

"Toronto," he murmured, savoring the word on his tongue like a sweet treat. The possibilities seemed endless in this foreign land.

Gurmeet leaned casually against the doorframe, her ponytail swinging slightly as she watched her husband with excitement. This leap into the unknown was daunting, but with Sukhdeep by her side, she felt steady and secure.

"Have you thought about where we should settle in Toronto?" Gurmeet asked softly, knowing that they would soon have to make important decisions.

Sukhdeep turned away from the globe, his attention shifting from the expansive world to the woman who captured his heart. He closed the distance between them, taking her hands in his.

"I've been researching different neighborhoods," he replied earnestly, "ones that would be convenient for work. But I also want it to feel like home for you and our children."

"Didi's sister called earlier," Gurmeet said with a smile, "She mentioned Brampton has a thriving Punjabi community. She thinks we would fit right in there."

"Brampton?" Sukhdeep repeated, trying to place the name among the many he had looked into.

"Yes," Gurmeet nodded eagerly, "She said it's like a little piece of Punjab. There are gurdwaras, Indian grocery stores, even Punjabi language classes for the kids."

Sukhdeep liked the idea of being close to so many cultural places, but he knew he had to think about other things, too. He took out his phone and searched for the address of the company where he would be working. A map appeared on the screen, showing the route with traffic signs and long travel times.

"Look at this, Gurmeet," Sukhdeep gestured towards the screen, tracing the path from Brampton to downtown Toronto with a doubtful finger. "It's quite far from work. The daily travel might wear me down."

"But think about the weekends, the festivals," Gurmeet countered, her eyes shining with hope. "We won't feel as homesick if we have a piece of Punjab right here with us."

"True," Sukhdeep conceded, torn between the convenience of a shorter commute and the warmth of cultural familiarity. "But coming home exhausted every day after work, when will I have time to enjoy all this?" His hand glided across the digital depiction of community and comfort on the screen.

"Maybe it's worth it? For us--for our children?" Gurmeet suggested softly, her desire to maintain their cultural ties evident in her earnest gaze.

"Or maybe there's a middle ground somewhere," Sukhdeep offered. He wanted to find a solution that would satisfy both of their needs.

"Somewhere we can have both--the community and a manageable commute."

Their conversation went back and forth, talking about the good and bad sides, their hopes, and the practical things they had to consider. They kept talking late into the night, trying to find the best place to live. In the end, they both knew that no matter where they moved, as long as they were together, it would feel like home.

The threads of immigration intricately weave the tapestry of global cities and communities. As immigrants' journey towards fresh prospects and an enhanced quality of life, their chosen neighborhoods become mirrors reflecting their desires, dreams, and needs while simultaneously enriching the social, economic, and cultural mosaic of these areas. How do these choices mold communities and offer a rich palette of examples, statistics, and facts from diverse international contexts?

The allure of economic prospects is a major factor in why immigrants choose certain neighborhoods. Many immigrants are frequently motivated by the promise of better employment and living conditions. Research indicates that immigrants gravitate toward areas with thriving labor markets that complement their skill sets (Borjas, 1994).

For example, in America's landscape, neighborhoods such as Los Angeles' Koreatown and New York City's Jackson Heights have evolved into hotspots for Asian immigrants. These areas' economic profiles are sculpted by immigrant-owned businesses that not only provide employment opportunities but also nurture cultural continuity (Ylanan & Kambhampati, 2024).

The role played by social networks in choosing a neighborhood is significant, too. A majority of immigrants favor areas inhabited by family members or individuals sharing their cultural background or friends. This pattern, known as "chain migration," instills a sense of belongingness while offering crucial support systems during settlement.

In Canada's Toronto cityscape, for instance - the Scarborough suburb has witnessed a considerable influx, especially from South Asia, due to pre-existing communities that simplify integration processes for newcomers besides facilitating resource access and job-hunting efforts (Ashley, 2021).

Another factor influencing immigrants' decisions on where to settle is housing affordability. Newcomers frequently have limited housing options due to financial restrictions, which causes them to choose communities with lower rents or purchase costs, even though these locations may lack amenities or services.

"Lack of affordable housing worldwide is becoming a global crisis. An estimated 1.6 billion people—one-fifth of humanity—lack access to adequate housing and basic services, according to the UN special rapporteur on the right to adequate housing, and this number could rise to 3 billion by 2030" (Solf, Guerrero, & Sherzad, 2024).

In cities like London, boroughs such as Barking and Dagenham have gained popularity among immigrants seeking affordable housing. These historically less affluent neighborhoods offer reduced rent rates, attracting newcomers. But this influx also triggers demographic changes impacting local economies and social dynamics (Smith, 2016).

Neighborhoods chosen by immigrants frequently evolve into cultural enclaves, allowing them to uphold their cultural identities while assimilating into wider society. These enclaves are characterized by businesses, eateries, and community centers that echo the cultural heritage of the residents.

Chicago's Pilsen neighborhood is one such example where a dynamic Mexican community has flourished over decades. Renowned for its street art, restaurants, and cultural festivals like the annual Día de los Muertos celebration. This fosters a sense of unity and belonging but also raises gentrification concerns due to escalating property values threatening the neighborhood's cultural fabric (Baker, 1995).

Immigrants significantly boost their chosen neighborhoods' local economy, often initiating businesses that create jobs and stimulate economic activity. "According to Business Development Bank of Canada (BDC), Canada's only bank devoted exclusively to entrepreneurs, immigrant entrepreneurship is becoming a major force in shaping Canada's economy" (BDC, 2024).

In San Francisco, neighborhoods like the Mission District have transformed into buzzing commercial hubs featuring immigrant-owned businesses catering to both locals and tourists. These enterprises not only generate employment opportunities but also enrich the community's cultural landscape.

A new report from the American Immigration Council found that as of 2024, 46% of all Fortune 500 companies were founded by immigrants or their children. It is the highest level recorded since Council researchers started tracking immigrant entrepreneurs in annual reviews since 2011.

"We know that immigrants are far more likely than U.S.-born Americans to start their own business. This generates a ripple effect of more opportunities and greater prosperity for our communities" (American immigration Council, 2024).

While immigrants enrich their communities, they may also encounter challenges impacting social cohesion. Issues like language barriers, cultural differences, and discrimination can obstruct integration, leading to tensions between immigrant and native populations.

In Germany, for instance, the assimilation of Syrian refugees has elicited both support and resistance within neighborhoods. Cities like Berlin have experienced a significant refugee influx, sparking cultural conflicts and debates over resource distribution. While community initiatives by many locals have offered support, others have voiced concerns regarding social services and housing availability. This ongoing dialogue about integration and cultural coexistence continues to shape these neighborhoods' dynamics (Hindy, 2018).

In numerous American cities, historic neighborhoods like New York City's Little Italy and San Francisco's Chinatown serve as prime examples of immigrant communities preserving cultural practices, foods, and traditions dating back generations. Despite gentrification challenges Little Italy remains a cultural symbol attracting tourists and locals alike even though its once significant Italian population has dwindled. Contrastingly, Chinatown has emerged as a vibrant hub for Chinese immigrants, offering an array of services, restaurants, and cultural events.

In the heart of North America, the Greater Toronto Area (GTA) stands as a testament to multiculturalism, with more than half of its inhabitants hailing from foreign shores. Areas like Brampton and Mississauga have transformed into cultural melting pots thanks to the steady stream of newcomers from South Asia, the Middle East, and Africa. As per Statistics Canada's 2021 report, Brampton now boasts over 200,000 residents of South Asian descent, marking an undeniable shift in both its cultural and economic fabric (Statistics Canada, 2021).

Community organizations provide a wide range of tools, including job placement services and language instruction, to assist these recent arrivals in settling in. In addition to improving local communities, this cultural blending has made GTA a global leader in diversity and creativity.

Across the Pacific Ocean in Sydney lies another city known for its diverse immigrant populations. Cabramatta and Harris Park have emerged as epicenters for Vietnamese and Indian communities, respectively. A Report revealed that nearly one-third of Sydney's inhabitants were born overseas - a significant portion from Asian countries (NSW, 2023).

Cabramatta is particularly renowned for its food culture that showcases Vietnamese cuisine in all its glory. Local businesses thrive here, adding to the area's economic vitality and cultural uniqueness. However, issues like crime and social tensions have surfaced over time, urging community leaders to foster dialogue and mutual understanding among residents (Chieng, 2018).

The environment of their new towns can be greatly influenced by the choices immigrants make about where to establish their roots. These decisions are influenced by things like housing affordability, social ties, and economic opportunities; the neighborhoods that arise frequently develop into thriving cultural centers that enhance the vibrancy and energy of urban areas.

While hurdles such as discrimination and integration persistently loom on the horizon, immigration's overall influence on community formation is predominantly positive - it fuels economic growth while encouraging cultural exchange and social resilience.

As cities worldwide continue to morph under this influence, comprehending immigrant settlement dynamics becomes crucial for policymakers, community leaders, and residents. By acknowledging immigrants' contributions and addressing their challenges head-on, communities can nurture inclusive environments that celebrate diversity while enhancing social cohesion.

Ultimately, the neighborhoods resulting from these settlement patterns reflect not only the immigrant's journey but also the intricate tapestry of the broader human experience.

Tall Hedges and Unfamiliar Faces

The cold metal of the house keys pressed against my palm as I unlocked the front door to our new home in Vancouver. A gust of crisp British Columbian air rushed in, sweeping away the remnants of uncertainty that had lingered like shadows around my family these past few years as the world battled with COVID-19.

"Look, Daddy, look!" My daughter's voice, shrill with excitement, cut through the silence of the empty living room as she ran toward the expansive backyard, her brother hot on her heels.

"It's huge!" he echoed, his eyes wide with wonder. "Can we get a dog now? You said when we have a big yard, right?"

I smiled as I watched them run through the tall grass, their laughter filling the open space with joy. I took a deep breath, feeling the stress of every move, we had made—from a small rental apartment—finally fading away.

"Finally," I whispered to myself, a promise taking root, "we're home."

The children chattered about where they would set up their swing set, where the imaginary dog would sleep, and how they could build snowmen when winter came. Their innocence was a balm to the restlessness that had marked our nomadic rhythm.

"Settle down," I called out, chuckling as they pretended not to hear me, already lost in plans for a treehouse among the autumn-kissed leaves.

I trailed my fingers along the cool, neutrally painted walls of the hallway, a silent homage to the blank canvas of our new life. The emptiness of the rooms echoed back at me, not with hollowness but with a symphony of potential. Each corner held whispers of future laughter and memories waiting to be etched into its very fibers.

My mind wandered across oceans and continents, from the vibrant markets of London buzzing with life to the refined elegance of Scotland's cobblestone streets. I remembered how The Hague's lush greenery seemed to cradle the city in an everlasting embrace. Each place had shaped me and molded my children's early years with diverse sights and sounds. Yet here, in this quiet expanse, I found an unexpected kinship with the stillness.

In contrast to the continuous noise of traffic and conversation that had been our constant companion in previous residences, the soft sway of the tall grass outside my window was a pleasant diversion. This was a place of calm where one could ponder and breathe without being overpowered by outside sounds.

"Look, Daddy!" My daughter's enthusiastic voice snapped me out of my trance as the kids burst through the door, their energy sweeping through the house like a gust of wind. They provided a stark contrast to the calm of the empty rooms, a reminder of the life that would soon occupy every nook and cranny.

"Can we explore? There's a park nearby! Maybe we'll make some friends," she said, her eyes gleaming with the same adventurous spirit that had kept us buoyant through all the moves.

"Of course," I replied, my heart swelling with pride at their resilience. "Let's see what adventures await us in our new neighborhood."

As we stepped out into the crisp Vancouver air, the soft crunch of autumn leaves underfoot filled me with a sense of promise. With each step towards the park, I watched my children skip ahead, their laughter carving a path to new beginnings.

Our leisurely walk down the sidewalk crunched through a bunch of fallen leaves. I offered warm smiles and lifted my hand in greeting neighbors tending their gardens or washing cars in driveways. They responded with friendly waves, some pausing to return the gesture with equal enthusiasm.

Around the corner, the park appeared, a verdant canvas surrounded by slides and swings that called out to my kids. They raced ahead, leaving behind the constant change of their previous lives. I sat down to keep *watch on them after finding an unoccupied bench with cool wooden slats against the fall chill.*

Squeals of delight rose above the ambient sounds of the neighborhood—the rhythmic creaking of swings, the soft thud of feet landing on the sand. I tracked my children as they climbed and descended, their figures blurring with others yet standing out to me like beacons of joy.

As I listened to the laughter and playful shouts, I looked around and suddenly realized something. There were no other faces like theirs, no mix of cultures like in our old neighborhoods. The people here were friendly, and the place was peaceful, but the diversity I had always loved was missing.

Leaning back, hands clasped together, I contemplated this new dynamic. What would it mean for us, for my children, to grow roots in a place where their heritage was an outlier? I watched them swing higher, unfazed, their spirits undimmed, and knew that, like all the other places before, we would find our way. We always did for home is where you choose to have it.

Finding a home within a cultural enclave presents immigrants with numerous advantages. A palpable benefit is the ready-made support system, a network of individuals who mirror your cultural background and experiences. These enclaves often act as lifelines for newcomers, offering vital resources like ethnic grocery stores, places of worship, and community centers.

Moreover, immersing oneself in an environment that mirrors one's homeland can significantly alleviate the stress associated with acclimatizing to a new country and protection from any prejudice or cultural hurdles. This connection often translates into improved mental health outcomes since individuals can lean on their community for support during trying times.

However, living within these cultural enclaves also has its downsides. While these neighborhoods offer familiarity, they can also limit exposure to broader societal interactions and opportunities.

Additionally, issues such as gentrification threaten the economic stability of long-standing residents when rising property values and rental costs come into play. For example, San Francisco's Mission District has seen many Latino families pushed out due to increased housing costs resulting from an influx of tech workers (Chin, Glavas, King, Yamamoto & Zhang, 2024).

On the other hand, choosing to settle amidst diverse cultures offers numerous benefits, like fostering greater cultural exchange and understanding. Cities like Toronto are celebrated for their multiculturalism, with over 50% of residents born outside of Canada. Neighborhoods such as Kensington Market and Parkdale are vibrant mosaics where diverse cultural practices and cuisines thrive (ICS News, 2023).

The choice of where immigrants settle—whether within cultural enclaves or amidst a blend of cultures—has profound implications for their experiences and the communities they join. Understanding these dynamics is crucial for policymakers and community leaders as they strive to create inclusive environments that embrace diversity while addressing immigrant challenges. By fostering dialogue across cultural divides, communities can enhance social cohesion and build an equitable future for all residents. The immigrant experience is complex, but with the right support, it can lead to enriched communities that celebrate diversity and promote mutual respect.

Chapter Ten- Global Plates, Local Palates

"Laughter is brightest in the place where the food is."

– Irish Proverb

New Food, New Experience

The chilled, frothy cappuccino slid through Amina's fingers, offering a refreshing contrast to the warm buzz of the cozy café nestled in the heart of the University of Chicago. She had claimed a small corner table, tucked away from the bustling crowd but still close enough to feel the pulse of student life around her. The aroma of freshly ground coffee beans mingled with the sound of light chatter and the gentle clinking of cups and plates.

Amina, whose journey from the sun-drenched streets of Sousse, Tunisia, to the vibrant academic halls of Chicago had been filled with both excitement and longing, now sat across from her newfound friend Afia. Afi's presence radiated an aura of thoughtful composure in every movement. As a PhD candidate from Kumasi, Afia carried the rich tapestry of Ghanaian culture within her; her studies in humanities wove together threads of history, language, and philosophy. Her dark eyes, always sparkling with curiosity, met Amina's with a warmth that conveyed volumes about their quickly blossoming friendship.

"Chicago winters will take some getting used to," Amina remarked, breaking the comfortable silence as she traced the condensation on her glass, thinking back to the warmer climes of Tunisia. Her voice held a hint of accent, the musicality of French-infused Arabic softened by her growing familiarity with English.

Afia laughed gently, her own accent a rhythmic melody that danced between their words. "I can only imagine. Kumasi may have its heavy rains, but snow is another matter entirely."

The two friends sat nestled in their corner table like two puzzle pieces fitting perfectly together. The low hum of conversation and laughter surrounded them as Amina reached across the table to offer Afia a packet of sugar for her coffee. Their second meeting felt as natural, as if they were old friends catching up after years apart.

"Do you remember the scavenger hunt during orientation week?" Amina asked, her eyes twinkling with amusement. "I've never seen anyone so determined to find that statue of the University's founder."

Afia chuckled, her laughter causing nearby students to glance over curiously. "Oh, I was on a mission! I couldn't let us newcomers show anything less than excellence." Her determination not only impressed Amina but also endeared her to her during that first university-organized event designed to foster connections among new students.

"Excellence indeed," Amina agreed, stirring her iced cappuccino. "But it was your passion for the stories behind each landmark that truly made our team stand out."

"Stories are everywhere," Afia said, a hint of philosophical reflection in her voice. "They're what connect us, don't you think? Whether through economics or the humanities, we're all trying to understand the narrative of human experience."

Amina nodded as her thoughts quickly strayed to the economic theories, she was keen to investigate and that might one day contribute to bettering living conditions in Sousse. "Of course. She pointed loosely to the window that overlooked the busy streets of Chicago and said, "It's like this city - full of so many stories intersecting and diverging, just waiting to be discovered and shared." Their voices blended in perfectly with the vibrant energy of the café as they moved from playful banter about their undergraduate adventures to thoughtful conversations about culture and identity.

"What is your favorite restaurant here?" Amina asked, her dark eyes sparkling with curiosity.

"Well, it used to be McDonald's," Afia replied, a faint smile tugging at the corners of her lips. "But lately, I've been getting into sushi."

"You didn't like it before?"

Afia shook her head, sandy brown curls bouncing around her face. "I had never eaten anything uncooked until recently."

Amina raised an eyebrow in surprise. "Never? Not even as a child?"

"Not in my hometown of Kumasi," Afia explained with a shrug. "We cook everything there. It's not just a preference; it's almost a cultural rule to have our food 'done well.'"

Amina chuckled, nodding in understanding. "Food can definitely be a reflection of our upbringing."

"Yes, it can," Afia agreed, taking a sip of her coffee.

"I remember having my own encounter with unfamiliar food back in Tunisia," Amina said, leaning forward and cradling her chilled drink.

"Oh?" Afia leaned in, intrigued by Amina's words.

"It was years ago," Amina began with a fond smile. "My sisters and I were watching an American movie, and these kids kept talking about PB&J sandwiches. We were so curious that we begged our father to let us try some peanut butter."

"And did you find any?" Afia asked, picturing the scene in her mind.

"We searched every aisle of our local market in Sousse," Amina recounted with a smile. "And finally, we found one lone jar tucked away on a bottom shelf, as if holding secrets from another world."

"A treasure hunt for an exotic item," Afia commented with amusement.

"Exactly," Amina nodded, her eyes glinting with excitement as she continued the story. "We brought the jar home like a prized possession and gathered around the kitchen table."

"Sounds like a special family moment," Afia smiled.

"It was," Amina agreed. *"We each had a spoon and eagerly opened the jar. But then we tasted it..."*

"And?" Afia leaned in, eager to hear the outcome.

"We were disappointed," Amina admitted with a giggle. *"It was so thick and dry; it stuck to the roof of our mouths. We had to reach for water after just one taste."*

"Culture shock comes in many forms," Afia laughed, relating to the experience of unfamiliar foods.

"Indeed," Amina nodded, her smile widening at the memory. *"And peanut butter seemed to lack one important thing - flavor."*

"So, no more peanut butter for you?" Afia teased, smiling.

"Well, actually..." Amina's smile grew wider. *"My American cousin converted me."*

"How did she manage that?" Afia asked, genuinely curious.

"She made it for me when I moved here," Amina explained with a grin. *"And she added some honey and banana slices...it made all the difference."* The genuine smile on her face was a silent admission of her newfound love for peanut butter.

Food, a universal language that transcends international borders, is more than a means of sustenance. It's a canvas painted with cultural identities, traditions, and communal bonds, illustrating the role food plays in shaping social interactions and bridging gaps between diverse cultures. The rituals involved in preparing, sharing, and consuming food are unique threads that weave the fabric of heritage and community ties. This narrative will traverse various global culinary landscapes, offering vivid examples and intriguing data to underscore how food nurtures connection and understanding among people from disparate backgrounds (UBC, 2024).

Consider the rich tapestry woven into Italian cuisine. Renowned for its emphasis on fresh, high-quality ingredients and regional specialties, Italian cooking resonates with familial connections – recipes are precious heirlooms passed down through generations. Traditional dishes like pasta, risotto, and pizza aren't just sources of nourishment; they're celebrations of cultural lineage.

An important part of Italian culture is Sunday dinners. Families gather around the table for multi-course feasts on these holidays, which strengthens family ties while preserving cultural identity (UBC, 2024).

On the other end of the spectrum lies Japanese cuisine with its focus on seasonality and aesthetics. The meticulous crafting of dishes such as sushi or kaiseki—a multi-course meal—showcases not only culinary prowess but also a profound appreciation for nature's rhythm and shifting seasons.

Japanese gastronomy mirrors mindfulness – it's a reflection of simplicity coupled with reverence for ingredients. "At the core of Japanese cuisine is the concept of harmony, known as "wa" in Japanese. Wa is the delicate balance and coexistence of contrasting elements - flavours, textures, colours, and even seasons - within a single meal. This principle is a constant, not only in the cuisine but in every aspect of Japanese life" (Culinary Journey, 2023).

"African cuisine is a testament to the continent's rich diversity, deeply rooted in centuries of tradition, culture, and history. From the aromatic spices of North Africa to the hearty stews of West Africa, each region boasts a distinctive culinary identity that reflects its unique landscape and heritage. This vast culinary tapestry is woven together by staple foods, which form the backbone of daily nourishment across the continent" (Adminm, 2024).

In Ethiopia, for instance, communal sharing of injera (a sourdough flatbread) and various stews (known as wot) is central to social gatherings. Meals are often served on a large platter, where everyone eats with their hands – an act that underscores unity and connection.

In Nigeria, dishes like jollof rice and suya (spicy grilled meat) play crucial roles in celebrations and family gatherings. The "Jollof Rice Battle," a friendly rivalry between West African nations over who makes the best jollof, showcases how food can ignite passion while reinforcing cultural identity (Victory Osahon, 2024).

Food also acts as a powerful catalyst for social interaction and community building. In Mexico, communal meals play a vital role in cultural celebrations. Dishes like tamales and pozole, made in large quantities during family gatherings or festivals, highlight the importance of sharing and unity (Garcia, 2025).

Middle Eastern cultures echo this sentiment of communal dining, where meals often transform into festive gatherings. Sharing dishes like mezze—a variety of small plates served before the main course—encourages hospitality among diners.

In many European cultures, food also serves as a conduit for connection. In France, for example, meals are considered an art form with an emphasis on multi-course dining that encourages conversation and enjoyment (Shariff, 2011).

In Spain, the cherished custom of tapas - petite plates to be passed among companions - cultivates a laid-back ambiance that encourages camaraderie and a sense of community. "The origins of tapas can be traced back to medieval Spain, where it is said that King Alfonso X of Castile ordered that a small plate of food be served with every drink in order to prevent his subjects from becoming overly drunk. This tradition eventually spread throughout Spain, and tapas became a staple of Spanish culture and cuisine." (Blog- What are Spanish Tapas?, 2023).

Food serves as a medium for storytelling, memory formation, and promoting unity in each of these civilizations. Sharing meals fosters deep links with one's heritage and with one another, whether it is through the Nigerian Jollof rice, the French culinary adventure, the Ethiopian injera spread, the Italian Sunday feast, or the traditional Japanese tea ceremony. Food's ability to bridge cultural divides is becoming more and more important as we navigate a world that is becoming more interconnected.

Food surpasses mere nourishment; it encapsulates our shared human experience and mirrors our collective identities. In an era where divisions often seem insurmountable, food's universal appeal serves as a beacon highlighting ties that bind us all together while fostering understanding and appreciation for diverse cultures. Through food, we celebrate not only our distinctions but also our commonalities, weaving a rich tapestry of human connection that enhances our existence.

Tea Room Whispers

Anaya settled herself into the plush velvet settee, her body enveloped in its warmth and comfort. As she exhaled a contented sigh, the tearoom seemed to wrap around her like a warm embrace.

To her left, Luningning's eyes danced with delight as she took in the intricate patterns of the china and the glimmering silverware. Across from them, Olivia sat with perfect posture, exuding an air of grace that could only come from years spent in England's idyllic countryside.

Olivia beamed, her accent adding a touch of familiarity to her words. The air was filled with the fragrant aroma of teas and freshly baked treats, intoxicating and indulgent. It spoke of tradition and a hint of luxury, transporting the trio to a world where time slowed enough for them to savor each bite and every sip.

Luningning leaned in closer, curiosity sparking in her eyes at this new experience. "I've never seen anything like this back home," she breathed in wonderment.

Anaya nodded eagerly, mirroring her friend's excitement. She had always dreamed of experiencing high tea, with its quaint customs and delicate treats. It felt like stepping into a different realm, one where every detail was savored, and nothing was rushed.

Olivia surveyed the room with pride before turning her gaze back to her companions. "High tea is more than just a meal; it's an experience," she declared, the soft clinking of porcelain signaling another table being served.

After a moment of hesitation, Anaya traced her finger down the list of teas on the elaborate menu in front of her. She thought that English Breakfast was a good choice for her first high tea because it was strong and simple, just like the willpower she brought to her daily work life. She nodded confidently, "English Breakfast for me," she declared.

Beside her, Luningning's eyes roamed over the selection, finally settling on a jasmine tea that reminded her of home. "Jasmine tea," she said softly, a smile playing on her lips as she imagined its floral fragrance taking her back to the peaceful gardens of her childhood.

In her element, Olivia needed no time to decide. "Earl Grey, please," she told the waiter with a self-assuredness born from years of enjoying the classic blend. Her love for tradition and nostalgia was unwavering.

As the waiter withdrew, the women leaned in eagerly towards their table filled with delicate finger sandwiches, scones, and clotted cream— a picturesque arrangement begging to be captured forever. Anaya reached for her phone, the camera lens capturing the intricate tiers of savory and sweet treats. The click of the shutter interrupted their laughter, freezing not just the food but also the essence of their shared joy.

"Let's make sure we get a photo of the scones, too," Olivia instructed, arranging the plate just so. "They're the crown jewel of any high tea."

Luningning adjusted her position, finding her best angle as she posed playfully with an artful arrangement of cucumber sandwiches. "Wait, let me do the 'tea influencer' pose," she giggled, holding up her cup with exaggerated elegance that had them all chuckling.

Anaya gently spread clotted cream on a scone before taking a delicate bite, contrasting with the hearty laughter that filled the air. The three friends sat comfortably nestled in their cushioned chairs, shielded from the outside world by their intimate gathering.

"Isn't it remarkable," Anaya remarked thoughtfully, balancing her saucer on one knee, "how at work we're always rushing to grab a coffee, but here we are fully immersed in the art of tea?"

Luningning nodded in agreement, her eyes sparkling above the rim of her jasmine tea cup. "It's like we're different people outside those office walls—maybe a bit more refined?" she mused with a smile."

"Or perhaps it's just that coffee fuels the workday," Olivia added with a wry smile, her fingers curled around her steaming cup of Earl Grey. The delicate aroma wafted up from the amber liquid, calming and invigorating at the same time. "While tea invites us to slow down and savor."

"True," Anaya agreed, setting down her empty teacup with a soft clink. "At home, we have chai. It's more than just a drink; it's a ritual." Her voice took on a dreamy quality as she remembered the comforting scent of cardamom and cinnamon swirling in her childhood kitchen. "We'd pair it with samosas, the spices mingling with the tea in perfect harmony. Each sip was like a dance of flavors on our tongues."

Luningning leaned forward, tracing the intricate floral pattern on the tablecloth with her finger as she spoke. The fabric felt cool and smooth against her skin, a contrast to the warmth of their conversation. "In the Philippines, tea isn't the traditional drink of choice," she confessed, tucking a stray lock of hair behind her ear. "But on special occasions, we would enjoy it with empanadas." She demonstrated by miming breaking one open, her gestures bringing to life the image of flaky pastry filled with savory meats or cheeses.

"Sounds delicious," Anaya said, picturing the bustling streets of Manila lined with food stalls and vendors selling these delectable treats.

"Absolutely," Luningning confirmed with an emphatic nod. "It's not an everyday thing, but when it happens, it's a moment to pause and indulge—a small luxury amidst our busy lives."

Olivia, who had been listening intently, now let a smile play on her lips, her eyes sparkling with the joy of discovery. "I guess drinking tea and enjoying snacks is a universal tradition, with each culture adding its own unique twist," she mused, her British accent wrapping around the words like a warm blanket. "But in the end, it all comes back to the simple pleasures—companionship, conversation, and good food." Her gaze swept over the array of treats before them, linking this foreign experience to her own roots.

Luningning and Anaya nodded in accord, their smiles recognizing the universal language of friendship that cut across boundaries—a silent toast to kinship and diversity, drunk from fragile teacups full of history. They experienced the depth of their cultures and the enduring power of their ties with every drink.

Laughter and Spices

Yemi's laughter bubbled up from deep within him, warm and infectious, as he reclined in his chair. His eyes glowed with lightheartedness and a mischievous spark. "Oh, you simply must hear this one, Lina," he exclaimed, motioning dismissively to the remnants of our international potluck dinner. The air was still filled with the fragrant scents of spices and herbs, a testament to our successful culinary adventure together.

"Picture this," Yemi began, taking on the role of a masterful storyteller with a captivated audience in me. "Bangalore, the heart of India's tech revolution. And for me, it became a lesson in humility."

Eager to be carried away by his recollections, Lina leaned forward and rested her chin on her hand. Lina didn't want to miss Yemi's ability to transform ordinary situations into magnificent stories, which she had always had.

"After living in the UK for years, I thought I knew Indian food like the back of my hand," he continued, his voice now tinged with a mix of playful arrogance and honest reflection. "Tikka masala, bhajis—I could eat them all day."

A smirk danced on Lina's lips. She knew this was going to be a good story.

"So, there I was, in this authentic Indian restaurant, confidently ordering from the menu." Yemi paused, shaking his head as if he could still see the waiter's puzzled expression. "And what did I do? With all the swagger of a man who had just passed his citizenship test with flying colors, I ordered 'Peshwari naan.'"

The reenactment of his own faux pas was spot-on, complete with a pompous lift of his chin and an exaggerated British accent that had grown stronger with each pint he had consumed during his time in the UK.

Yemi's expression shifted as he remembered the waiter's reaction, a mix of fondness and chagrin. "The poor guy looked at me as if I had requested a unicorn on a platter. He leaned in close, his eyebrows furrowed with concern and apologized." Yemi lowered his voice to mimic the server's gentle tone. "'Sir, we have butter naan, plain naan... but Peshwari naan?'" We don't make that here." My heart sank. Years of relishing what I thought was authentic Indian cuisine, and here I was, utterly wrong-footed.

What I discovered was both enlightening and amusing: Peshawari naan actually hails from Peshawar, a region in Pakistan. Could you imagine my shock as I realised I had been asking an Indian waiter for Pakistani food? All these years I had been encountering a remix tailored to British tastes.

Lina couldn't contain her laughter any longer, and it blended seamlessly with Yemi's hearty chuckles.

"Needless to say," Yemi concluded, grinning from ear to ear, "I learned that day that having a taste for something doesn't mean you know it all. And that, my friend, is the beauty of traveling—and eating—outside your comfort zone."

Lina clasped her thin fingers around her steaming cup and leaned forward, her eyes glimmering with the promise of a story. Her tea's reassuring aroma filled the room as it drifted between us.

"Your naan story reminds me of my own culinary misadventure," she began, a playful smirk tugging at the corners of her mouth. "It was just after I'd moved to Montreal from Jordan. In Amman during the '90s, Chinese cuisine was this exotic rarity served in hushed, fancy restaurants." She paused for a moment, lost in the recollection, and then continued with a faint sigh. "So, there I was, in this bustling Canadian city, eager to blend in with my new friends who suggested we go out for some 'authentic' Chinese food." The way she said 'authentic,' with air quotes and an exaggerated nod, made it clear that her definition had since expanded.

"We ended up at this vibrant spot downtown. Red lanterns swayed above us, casting a warm glow over our table as the scent of spices hung heavy in the air—nothing like the quiet elegance of the places back home." She shook her head, laughing softly at the memory.

"I scanned the menu, looking for anything familiar. And there it was: General Tao's chicken. I ordered it with such confidence, only to be

presented with a dish that looked nothing like the sweet, sticky morsels I remembered."

"Was it terrible?" Yemi asked, leaning in closer, drawn into her story.

"Quite the opposite," Lina replied, her voice filled with surprise and delight.

"It was this delightful explosion of flavors—spicy, tangy, slightly sweet. Nothing like the General Tao I knew, but delicious in its own right. It taught me to embrace the unexpected, especially when it comes to food,"

We shared a knowing look, acknowledging our mutual journey of culinary enlightenment. Just then, Yemi let out a hearty laugh, waving his hand as if to draw a line under our shared anecdotes.

"Alright, alright," he chuckled, his eyes twinkling with mischief.

"I think we've established that we're both champions at diving into the deep end of the dining pool. But remember, the next time you order an authentic dish, there's a whole world of flavors waiting to surprise you." A wink punctuated his words, and Lina couldn't help but join in the laughter.

"Surprise being the key word," Lina added, raising my glass in a toast to our international palates and the adventures yet to come. Each sip of tea brought a new burst of warmth and flavor, mirroring the unexpected twists and turns of life's culinary adventures.

References

Introduction

International Organization for Migration. (2024). *World migration report 2024*. International Organization for Migration. https://publications.iom.int/books/world-migration-report-2024

United Nations. (n.d.). *International Migration 2020 Highlights | United Nations.* https://www.un.org/en/desa/international-migration-2020-highlights#:~:text=Among%20the%20major%20regions%20of,total%20of%20nearly%2050%20million

Chapter One

Bertrand, M., & Mullainathan, S. (2004). Are Emily and Greg more employable than Lakisha and Jamal? A field experiment on labor market discrimination. *American Economic Review, 94*(4), 991–1013. https://doi.org/10.1257/0002828042002561

Blum, S. D. (1997). Naming practices and the power of words in China. *Language in Society, 26*(3), 357–379. https://doi.org/10.1017/S0047404500021001

Carneiro, P., Lee, S., & Reis, H. (2019). Please call me John: Name choice and the assimilation of immigrants in the United States, 1900–1930. *Labour Economics, 62*, 101778. https://doi.org/10.1016/j.labeco.2019.101778

Deloitte Insights. (2017). *Diversity and inclusion at the workplace: A review of research and perspectives.* https://www2.deloitte.com/us/en/insights/focus/human-capital-trends/2017/diversity-and-inclusion-at-the-workplace.html

FamilySearch. (n.d.). *India naming customs.* FamilySearch. https://www.familysearch.org/en/wiki/India_Naming_Customs

Hawana, S. A. (1977). *Naming in Arabic* (Master's thesis). Iowa State University. https://dr.lib.iastate.edu/server/api/core/bitstreams/4279007e-e8ad-4f27-ad6d-606c2f68c786/content

Herring, C. (2009). Does diversity pay?: Race, gender, and the business case for diversity. *American Sociological Review, 74*(2), 208–224. https://doi.org/10.1177/000312240907400203

Kurt, D. (2025, February 3). *Corporate leadership by race.* Investopedia. https://www.investopedia.com/corporate-leadership-by-race-5114494

Malhotra, R. T. (2019, June 28). *How to reduce personal bias when hiring. Harvard Business Review.* https://hbr.org/2019/06/how-to-reduce-personal-bias-when-hiring

McKinsey & Company. (2020). *Diversity wins: How inclusion matters.* https://www.mckinsey.com/featured-insights/diversity-and-inclusion/diversity-wins-how-inclusion-matters

Mensah, E. O., Inyabri, I. T., & Nyong, B. O. (2020). Names, naming, and the code of cultural denial in a contemporary Nigerian society: An Afrocentric perspective. *Journal of Black Studies, 52*(3), 248–276. https://doi.org/10.1177/0021934720980097

Powers, A. (2018, June 27). A study finds that diverse companies produce 19% more revenue. *Forbes.* https://www.forbes.com/sites/annapowers/2018/06/27/a-study-finds-that-diverse-companies-produce-19-more-revenue/

Quillian, L., Lee, J. J., & Oliver, M. (2020). Evidence from field experiments in hiring shows substantial additional racial discrimination after the callback. *Social Forces, 99*(2), 732–759. https://doi.org/10.1093/sf/soaa026

Tague, R. (2019, February 15). *Native American naming traditions. Ethnic Technologies.* https://www.ethnictechnologies.com/blog/2018/10/2/native-american-naming-traditions

Tague, R. (2019, February 15). *Naming traditions from around the world. Ethnic Technologies.* https://www.ethnictechnologies.com/blog/2018/10/2/naming-traditions-from-around-the-world

U.S. Equal Employment Opportunity Commission. (n.d.). *Equal Employment Opportunity Commission research and data plan.* https://www.eeoc.gov/equal-employment-opportunity-commission-research-and-data-plan

U.S. Language Services LLC. (2024, October 10). *Naming traditions across cultures and languages. U.S. Language Services.* https://www.uslanguageservices.com/blog/naming-traditions-across-cultures-and-languages/

Ziegert, J. C., & Hanges, P. J. (2005). Employment discrimination: The role of implicit attitudes, motivation, and a climate for racial bias. *Journal of Applied Psychology, 90*(3), 553–562. https://doi.org/10.1037/0021-9010.90.3.553

Chapter Two

Boroditsky, L. (2001). Does language shape thought? Linguistic relativity and its consequences. In D. Gentner & S. Goldin-Meadow (Eds.), *Language in mind: Advances in the study of language and thought* (pp. 63–79). MIT Press. Retrieved from https://www.sciencedirect.com/journal/cognitive-psychology/vol/43/issue/1

Cherry, K. (2023). The Sapir-Whorf hypothesis: How language influences thinking. *Verywell Mind.* https://www.verywellmind.com/the-sapir-whorf-hypothesis-7565585

Diaz Olson, D. (2024). *Culture clash: Investigating interpersonal challenges between international and Dutch students.* University of Twente. Retrieved from https://essay.utwente.nl/101753/1/DiazOlson_BA_faculty.pdf.pdf

Hall, E. T. (1976). *Beyond culture.* Anchor Books. Retrieved from https://books.google.ca/books?hl=en&lr=&id=reByw3FWVWsC&oi=fnd&pg=PA1

Hedderich, N. (2010). *German-American inter-cultural differences at the workplace: A survey.* Purdue University. Retrieved from https://docs.lib.purdue.edu/cgi/viewcontent.cgi?article=1028&context=gbl

Kuiper, A. (2008). Review: *Intercultural communication: A contextual approach* (3rd ed.), by James W. Neuliep.

Business Communication Quarterly, 71(4), 516–518.
https://doi.org/10.1177/1080569908321864

La Cañada High School. (2023, March 10). *Guugu Yimithirr: A language feature. L.A. Times High School Insider.*
https://highschool.latimes.com/la-canada-high-school/guugu-yimithirr-a-language-feature/

Larina, T. (n.d.). *Category of politeness and communication style: Comparative analysis of English and Russian tradition. Across Languages and Cultures.* Retrieved from
https://d1wqtxts1xzle7.cloudfront.net/32753905/Accross_Languages_and_Cultures.pdf

LinguaLink DC. (2023, February 20). *U.S. culture: The art of small talk. LinguaLink DC Blog.*
https://www.lingualinkdc.net/blog/usculture-smalltalk

Livermore, D. (2013). *Expand your borders: Discover 10 cultural clusters.* Cultural Intelligence Center.

NTNU. (2024, July 15). *Language affects how quickly we perceive shades of colour. Norwegian SciTech News.*
https://norwegianscitechnews.com/2024/07/language-affects-how-quickly-we-perceive-shades-of-colour/

Nishimura, S., Nevgi, A., & Tella, S. (2008). *Communication style and cultural features in high/low context communication cultures: A case study of Finland, Japan and India.* Aalto University.
https://mycourses.aalto.fi/pluginfile.php/1189342/mod_resource/content/3/nishimuranevgitella299.pdf

Pavlenko, A. (2005). Bilingualism and emotions. *International Journal of Bilingualism, 9*(3–4), 391–410. https://doi.org/10.1177/13670069050090030401

Pew Research Center. (2021). *Politeness and communication styles in North America.* Retrieved from https://www.pewresearch.org

Schneider, K. P., & Placencia, M. E. (2017). *(Im)politeness and regional variation.* Birkbeck Institutional Research Online. Retrieved from https://eprints.bbk.ac.uk/id/eprint/14775/3/14775.pdf

Winawer, J., Witthoft, N., Frank, M. C., Wu, L., & Boroditsky, L. (2007). Russian blues reveal effects of language on color discrimination. *Proceedings of the National Academy of Sciences, 104*(19), 7780–7785. https://doi.org/10.1073/pnas.0701644104

Chapter Three

Alshihry, M. A. (2024). *Heritage language maintenance among immigrant youth: Factors influencing proficiency and identity.*

Alzayed, N. N. Y. (2015). *Preserving immigrants' native language and cultural identity in multilingual and multicultural societies.* Retrieved from https://d1wqtxts1xzle7.cloudfront.net/48490154/preserving_immigrant_native_language-libre.pdf

American Psychological Association. (2008). *Schools' resources important for helping children of immigrant families succeed in the classroom.* Retrieved from https://www.apa.org/news/press/releases/2008/11/immigrant-families

Greene, M., & Batalova, J. (2024). *Indian immigrants in the United States.* Migration Policy Institute. Retrieved from https://www.migrationpolicy.org/article/indian-immigrants-united-states

Lopez, M. H., Krogstad, J. M., & Flores, A. (2018). *Most Hispanic parents speak Spanish to their children, but this is less the case in later immigrant generations.* Pew Research Center. Retrieved from https://www.pewresearch.org/short-reads/2018/04/02/most-hispanic-parents-speak-spanish-to-their-children-but-this-is-less-the-case-in-later-immigrant-generations/

Poole, A. (2019, December 6). *Immigrants, their languages, and their children. Language Magazine.* Retrieved from https://www.languagemagazine.com/resources-immigrants-their-languages-and-their-children/

Ramirez-Esparza, N., & Garcia-Sierra, A. (2014). *The bilingual brain: Language, culture, and identity*. Retrieved from https://books.google.ca/books?hl=en&lr=&id=CQrVAwA AQBAJ&oi=fnd&pg=PA35

Rohani, S., Choi, C., Amjad, R. N., Burnett, C., & Colahan, C. (2006). *Language maintenance and the role of the family amongst immigrant groups in the United States: Persian-speaking Bahá'ís, Cantonese, Urdu, Spanish, and Japanese— An exploratory study*. Retrieved from https://d1wqtxts1xzle7.cloudfront.net/71791824/3280_La nguageMaintenanceandtheRoleoftheFamily-libre.pdf

Statistics Canada. (2016). Language. Retrieved from https://www150.statcan.gc.ca/n1/pub/11-402-x/2012000/chap/lang/lang-eng.htm

Thomas, W. P., & Collier, V. P. (2001). *A national study of school effectiveness for language minority students' long-term academic achievement*. Center for Research on Education, Diversity & Excellence. Retrieved from https://escholarship.org/content/qt65j213pt/qt65j213pt.p df?t=krnd6g

Vigdor, J. L. (2008). *Measuring immigrant assimilation in the United States*. Retrieved from https://www.policyarchive.org/handle/10207/11619

Villa, D. (2002). *Integrating technology into minority language preservation and teaching efforts: An inside job. Language Learning & Technology, 6.* Retrieved from https://www.researchgate.net/publication/249931611_Integrating_technology_into_minority_langugage_preservation_and_teaching_efforts_An_inside_job

Waters, M. C., & Pineau, M. G. (2015). *The integration of immigrants into American society: A report.* Retrieved from https://books.google.ca/books?hl=en&lr=&id=LZTRCwAAQBAJ&oi=fnd&pg=PR1

Chapter Four

Abdul-Zahra, S. (2010). *Code-switching in language: An applied study.* Retrieved from
https://www.iraqoaj.net/iasj/download/75523051ca7c4c8e

Australian Bureau of Statistics. (2016). *Census: Multicultural.* Retrieved from
https://www.abs.gov.au/ausstats/abs@.nsf/lookup/media%20release3

Brenda. (2020). *6 pronunciation mistakes Spanish speakers make in English (and how to fix them). Oxford House.* Retrieved from
https://oxfordhousebcn.com/en/6-pronunciation-mistakes-spanish-speakers-make-in-english-and-how-to-fix-them/

British Accent Academy. (n.d.). *Understanding pronunciation challenges for Arabic speakers.* Retrieved from
https://www.britishaccentacademy.com/most-common-english-pronunciation-errors-made-by-arabic-speakers/

Brusa, A., & Proverbio, A. M. (n.d.). *Voices and prejudice: Accent-based information affects the perceived competence and social attractiveness of the speaker.* Retrieved from
https://scholar.google.ca/scholar?hl=en&as_sdt=0%2C5&q=Perception+and+prejudice%3A+The+impact+of+accent+on+social+evaluations&btnG=

Coppinger, L., & Sheridan, S. (2022). *Accent anxiety: An exploration of non-native accent as a source of speaking anxiety among English as a foreign language (EFL) students. Journal for the Psychology of Language Learning.* Retrieved from

https://www.jpll.org/index.php/journal/article/download/9
3/99/589

Derwing, T. M. (2008). *Putting accent in its place: Rethinking
obstacles to communication.* Retrieved from
https://www.researchgate.net/publication/231831876_Putt
ing_accent_in_its_place_Rethinking_obstacles_to_commu
nication

Goatley-Soan, S., & Baldwin, J. R. (2018). *Words apart: A study of
attitudes toward varieties of South African English accents in
a United States employment scenario. Journal of Language
and Social Psychology, 37(6)*, 692–705.
https://doi.org/10.1177/0261927X18800129

Huang, L., Frideger, M., & Pearce, J. L. (2014). *How non-native
speakers can crack the glass ceiling. Harvard Business Review.*
Retrieved from https://hbr.org/2014/06/how-non-native-
speakers-can-crack-the-glass-ceiling

Kirkpatrick, A. (2010). *The Routledge handbook of world Englishes.*
Routledge. Retrieved from
https://www.taylorfrancis.com/chapters/edit/10.4324/9781
003128755-12/development-english-language-india-
joybrato-mukherjee-tobias-bernaisch

Kozlowski, A. (2015). *The influence of accents on social perception.*
Retrieved from
https://engime.org/pars_docs/refs/91/90903/90903.pdf

Luzzi, E. (2020). *Received pronunciation group report.* Retrieved
from

https://research.library.kutztown.edu/cgi/viewcontent.cgi?p
arams=/context/english334/article/1001/&path_info=Rece
ived_Pronunciation.pdf

Lyons, D. (2021). *How many people speak English, and where is it spoken? Babbel.* Retrieved from https://www.babbel.com/en/magazine/how-many-people-speak-english-and-where-is-it-spoken

Myles, J., & Cheng, L. (2003). *The social and cultural life of non-native English speaking international graduate students at a Canadian university. Journal of English for Academic Purposes, 2(3),* 247–263. https://doi.org/10.1016/S1475-1585(03)00028-6

Nurmia, N., & Koroma, J. (2020). *The emotional benefits and performance costs of building a psychologically safe language climate in MNCs. Journal of International Business Studies.* Retrieved from https://www.sciencedirect.com/science/article/pii/S109095 1620300213

Ouanhlee, T. (2024). *Effect on non-native English speakers of utilizing English for business. International Business Research, 16(9),* 16–16. https://doi.org/10.5539/ibr.v16n9p16

Śliwa, M., & Johansson, M. (2014). *How non-native English speaking staff are evaluated in linguistically diverse organizations: A sociolinguistic perspective. Journal of International Business Studies.* Retrieved from https://repository.essex.ac.uk/10803/1/JIBS%20Sliwa%20J ohansson%20accepted%20version.pdf

Chapter Five

Berger, R., Herstein, R., Silbiger, A., & Barnes, B. (2017). Developing international business relationships in a Russian context. *Management International Review, 57*(3), 441-471. https://shura.shu.ac.uk/13131/1/Barnes%20Developing%20International%20Business%20Relationships%20in%20a%20Russian%20Context.pdf

Bradshaw, R. (2024). *15 important networking statistics everyone should know.* Apollo Technical. https://www.apollotechnical.com/networking-statistics/#:~:text=80%25%20of%20professionals%20find%20networking,networking%20is%20to%20your%20career

Burhan, Q., & Malik, M. F. (2024). Concept of workplace camaraderie: Developing and testing an integrated model leading to incivility. *International Journal of Conflict Management, 35*(3), 453-470. https://doi.org/10.1108/IJCMA-05-2023-0090

Canadian Centre for Diversity and Inclusion. (2019). *National diversity and inclusion benchmarking study: Senior leaders and diversity personnel.* Dalhousie University. https://ccdi.ca/media/1979/20190715-research-national-diversity-and-inclusion-benchmarking-study.pdf

Dulworth, M. (2009). *The connect effect: Building strong personal, professional, and virtual networks.* Berrett-Koehler Publishers. https://www.bkconnection.com/static/The-Connect-Effect-EXCERPT.pdf

Japanese Business Culture and Practices. (2018). *Japanese business culture and practices (2nd ed.).* Isao Takeri & Jon P. Alston. https://books.google.ca/books?hl=en&lr=&id=ZBBfDwAAQBAJ&oi=fnd&pg=PT10&dq=Business+etiquette+in+Japan:+A+guide+to+networking&ots=WZISL6SKwk&sig=spH3jprN9op-KklBF5ouWoHI77Q#v=onepage&q&f=false

Livermore, D. (2013). *Expand your borders – Discover 10 cultural clusters.* CQ Press.

Molinsky, A. (2012). How to network across cultures. *Harvard Business Review.* https://hbr.org/2012/01/how-to-network-across-cultures

National Identity and Global Sports Events. (2006). *National identity and global sports events.* A. Tomlinson & C. Young (Eds.). Routledge. https://books.google.ca/books?hl=en&lr=&id=PhgDpnDoRYYC&oi=fnd&pg=PP9&dq=national+identity+and+sports.&ots=LpPQ1qqWNy&sig=EZcWw-7ky-7AoXFD1pUSCaNXPs8#v=onepage&q=national%20identity%20and%20sports.&f=false

Networking Statistics. (n.d.). *Networking statistics: General stats, benefits, face-to-face, and more!* TeamStage. https://teamstage.io/networking-statistics/

Nielsen. (2023). *Super Bowl viewership transcends platforms and devices.* https://www.nielsen.com/insights/2023/super-bowl-viewership-transcends-platforms-and-devices/

Tobar, F., & Gusso, L. (2017). Becoming Brazilian: The making of national identity through football. *The International Journal of Sport and Society, 8*(2), 37-49. https://www.researchgate.net/publication/317162394_Becoming_Brazilian_The_Making_of_National_Identity_through_Football/citation/download

Whyno, S. (2024). Steady decline in youth hockey participation in Canada raises concerns about sport's future. *CBC News.* https://www.cbc.ca/sports/hockey/youth-hockey-canada-declining-participation-1.7231607#:~:text=Definitely%20before%20the%20pandemic%20you,in%20Canada%20have%20already%20recovered.&text=%22I%27m%20concerned%20but%20I,the%20sake%20of%20the%20sport.%22

Agcaoili, L. (2024). How the rise of Premier Volleyball League has put volleyball on a pedestal in the Philippines. *Philippine Daily Inquirer.* https://asianews.network/how-the-rise-of-premier-volleyball-league-has-put-volleyball-on-a-pedestal-in-the-philippines/#:~:text=%E2%80%9CVolleyball%20is%20now%20the%20number,in%20the%20Philippines%2C%20not%20basketball.

Chapter Six

Ambady, N., & Rosenthal, R. (1992). Thin slices of nonverbal behavior as predictors of interpersonal consequence: A meta-analysis. *Psychological Bulletin, 111*(2), 256-274. https://courses.media.mit.edu/2004fall/mas921/Ambady%20Rosenthal%201992.pdf

Camilleri, A. P. (2024). Talking to strangers: A mixed-methods evaluation study of an intercultural intervention. *College of Science and Health Theses and Dissertations, 522.* https://via.library.depaul.edu/csh_etd/522

Cultural etiquette. (n.d.). *eDiplomat.* http://www.ediplomat.com/np/cultural_etiquette/cultural_etiquette.htm

Edward T. Hall, Proxemic Theory, 1966. (2001). *CSISS Classics – Brown, N.* https://escholarship.org/uc/item/4774h1rm

Ghanaian culture: A collection of useful pointers. (2018). *Ashley Young.* https://ieo.ucla.edu/ghana-ghanaian-culture-a-collection-of-useful-pointers/

Hall, E. T. (1966). *Proxemic theory.* CSISS Classics.

Horowitz, L. M., & Strack, S. (Eds.). (2010). *Handbook of interpersonal psychology: Theory, research, assessment, and therapeutic interventions.* Wiley. https://doi.org/10.1002/9781118001868.ch11

Ibrahim, N. A. N., Rani, N. S. A., Jamri, M. H., Bakar, M. H., Wahab, S. A., Mahbob, M. H., & Kahar, N. (2022). The importance of non-verbal communication in organizations. *International Journal of Academic Research in Business and Social Sciences, 12*(6). http://dx.doi.org/10.6007/IJARBSS/v12-i6/13901

Livermore, D. (2013). *Expand your borders – Discover 10 cultural clusters.* CQ Press.

Matsumoto, D. (2006). *Culture and nonverbal behavior.* https://www.davidmatsumoto.com/content/Matsumoto%20Chapter%2012%20Pages%20from%20Manusov%20II%20Proff-14.pdf

Pease, B., & Pease, A. (2008). *The definitive book of body language: The hidden meaning behind people's gestures and expressions.* Bantam Books. https://books.google.ca/books?hl=en&lr=&id=z5d_8bAyW8AC&oi=fnd&pg=PR14&dq=Cultural+expressions+of+body+language+in+Canada&ots=JON4jG3JSH&sig=axdF39ezaZyxAWTGPCN1U3UPm7Q#v=onepage&q=Cultural%20expressions%20of%20body%20language%20in%20Canada&f=false

UT Permian Basin. (n.d.). How much of communication is nonverbal? *UTPB Online BA in Communication Program.* https://online.utpb.edu/about-us/articles/communication/how-much-of-communication-is-nonverbal/#:~:text=The%2055/38/7%20Formula,%2C%20and%207%25%20words%20only.

Van Edwards, V. (2024). *The ultimate guide to making a great first impression (even online).* Science of People. https://www.scienceofpeople.com/first-impressions/

Zaharna, R. S. (1995). Understanding cultural preferences of Arab communication patterns. *American University.* https://www.american.edu/soc/faculty/upload/understanding-cultural-preferences-on-arab.pdf

Chapter Seven

Baur, J. (2020, May 31). What makes Germans so orderly? *BBC Travel.* https://www.bbc.com/travel/article/20200531-what-makes-germans-so-orderly

Heffernan, M. (2014, April 4). Why do success and punctuality go together? *CBS News.* https://www.cbsnews.com/news/why-do-success-and-punctuality-go-together/

Hofstede, G. (1983). Dimensions of national culture in fifty countries and three regions. In J. B. Deregowski, S. Dziurawiec, & R. C. Annis (Eds.), *Explanations in cross-cultural psychology* (pp. 335-355). Swets & Zeitlinger.

Livermore, D. (2013). *Expand your borders – Discover 10 cultural clusters.* CQ Press.

Rygg, K. (2012). *Direct and indirect communicative styles – A study.* https://openaccess.nhh.no/nhh-xmlui/bitstream/handle/11250/164267/rygg%20avh2012.pdf?sequence=1

Triandis, H. C. (1995). *Individualism & collectivism.* Westview Press. https://psycnet.apa.org/record/1995-97791-000

World Values Survey. (2021). *Wave 7: 2017-2020.* Retrieved from https://www.worldvaluessurvey.org/WVSDocumentation WV7.jsp

Chapter Eight

Akkoyun, A. G. (2024). *Perspective chapter: The Norwegian model of correlation rehabilitation – Bridging the gap between incarceration and society.* IntechOpen. https://www.intechopen.com/chapters/1178111

Assembly of First Nations (AFN). (2024). *Calls for a national inquiry into systemic racism in policing [Press release].* https://afn.ca/all-news/press-releases/assembly-of-first-nations-afn-calls-for-a-national-inquiry-into-systemic-racism-in-policing/

Brown, R. (2023). *Do we trust the police?* Psychology Today. https://www.psychologytoday.com/ca/blog/understanding-health-behaviors/202303/do-we-trust-the-police#:~:text=The%20Global%20Trustworthiness%20Index%20compares,addressing%20concerns%20about%20police%20culture

Conde-Brooks, P. (2023). *Personalismo drives Latino leadership by promoting a more inclusive and participatory leadership style.* LinkedIn. https://www.linkedin.com/pulse/personalismo-drives-latino-leadership-promoting-more-patricia/

Gashaw, T. T. (2017). *Colonial borders in Africa: Improper design and its impact on African borderland communities.* Wilson Center. https://www.wilsoncenter.org/blog-post/colonial-borders-in-africa-improper-design-and-its-impact-on-african-borderland-communities#:~:text=Besides%20improperly%20designed%20borders%2C%20European,this%20division%20for%20political%20means

Hallman Jecic, S. (2024). *Mutual trust - Community policing as a trust-building method in a Swedish police context.* https://www.diva-portal.org/smash/get/diva2:1449536/FULLTEXT01.pdf

Hofstede Insights. (n.d.). *Country comparison tool.* https://www.hofstede-insights.com/country-comparison/

Humans Rights Watch. (2021). *Nigeria: A year on, no justice for #EndSARS crackdown - Prosecute those responsible for abusing protesters.* https://www.hrw.org/news/2021/10/19/nigeria-year-no-justice-endsars-crackdown

Japan Dev Team. (2024). *Job titles and company positions in Japan: A complete guide.* https://japan-dev.com/blog/company-positions-and-job-titles-in-japanese#why-knowing-company-positions-and-job-titles-in-japanese-is-important

Meyer, E. (2017). *Being the boss in Brussels, Boston, and Beijing: If you want to succeed, you'll need to adapt.* Harvard Business Review. https://hbr.org/2017/07/being-the-boss-in-brussels-boston-and-beijing

Mutahi, P., Höglund, K., & Elfversson, E. (2024). *Policing and citizen trust in Kenya: How community policing shapes local trust-building and collaboration.* Uppsala University. https://uu.diva-portal.org/smash/get/diva2:1896390/FULLTEXT01.pdf

Statistics Norway. (n.d.). *Offences and victims reported to the police.*
https://www.ssb.no/en/sosiale-forhold-og-
kriminalitet/statistikker/lovbrudda/aar

Trading Economics. (2025). *Sweden - School enrollment, tertiary (%
gross) [Data sourced from the World Bank].*
https://tradingeconomics.com/sweden/school-enrollment-
tertiary-percent-gross-wb-
data.html#:~:text=School%20enrollment%2C%20tertiary
%20(%25%20gross)%20in%20Sweden%20was%20repor
ted%20at,compiled%20from%20officially%20recognized
%20sources

Tran, K. (2017). *How Japan's cultural norms affect policing: A side-
by-side comparison with the United States.* San José State
University.
https://scholarworks.sjsu.edu/cgi/viewcontent.cgi?article=1
051&context=themis

U.S. Department of State. (2022). *Country reports on human rights
practices.* https://www.state.gov/wp-
content/uploads/2023/02/415610_BRAZIL-2022-
HUMAN-RIGHTS-REPORT.pdf

Waghmare, A. (2024). *Education levels in India.* Data for India.
https://www.dataforindia.com/education-levels-in-india/

Chapter Nine

American Immigration Council. (2024). *New report shows how immigrant entrepreneurs create jobs across the U.S.* https://www.americanimmigrationcouncil.org/news/fortun e-500-2024-report-immigrant-entrepreneurs-create-jobs- across-united-states

Asian American Federation. (2008). *Revitalizing Chinatown businesses: Challenges and opportunities.* https://www.aafederation.org/doc/RevitalizingChinatownB usinesses.pdf

Ashley, R. (2021). *The gentrification of Scarberia.* This Magazine. https://this.org/2021/07/12/the-gentrification-of-scarberia/

Baker, A. (1995). *The social production of space of two Chicago neighborhoods: Pilsen and Lincoln Park.* ProQuest. https://www.proquest.com/openview/a07fa870a77d6c6c3f 0d4e05a3a9f272/1?pq- origsite=gscholar&cbl=18750&diss=y

Borjas, G. J. (1994). *The economics of immigration. Journal of Economic Literature, 32*(4), 1667-1717. https://www.aeaweb.org/articles/pdf/doi/10.1257/jel.2015 1248

Cabramatta, S. C. (2018). *Cabramatta: The taste, the people, the rep.* Medium. https://medium.com/@stephen_chieng/cabramatta-the- taste-the-people-the-rep-9f00497c0452

Chin, E., Glavas, J. A., King, K. A., Yamamoto, M. J., & Zhang, J. (2024). *Gentrification in Mission District, San Francisco.* ArcGIS StoryMaps. https://storymaps.arcgis.com/stories/9bfaaf0c5b4d4dcd9d 58abeb40667ad7

Goodey, J. (2009). *Immigrants as crime victims in the European Union: With special attention to hate crime.* In W. F. McDonald (Ed.), *Immigration, crime and justice* (Vol. 13, pp. 147-161). Emerald Group Publishing Limited. https://doi.org/10.1108/S1521-6136(2009)0000013012

Hindy, L. (2018). *Germany's Syrian refugee integration experiment.* The Century Foundation. https://tcf.org/content/report/germanys-syrian-refugee-integration-experiment/

ICS News. (2023). *ICS 2023 Toronto – Canada's multicultural hub.* https://www.ics.org/news/1366#:~:text=Toronto%20is%2 0one%20of%20the,almost%20as%20many%20languages %20&%20dialects.

Kauffman Foundation. (2022). *The role of immigrants in entrepreneurship.* https://www.kauffman.org/wp-content/uploads/2019/12/kauffman_compilation_immigra tion_entrepreneurship.pdf

NSW Government. (2023). *Multicultural demographics data explorer.* https://www.cancer.nsw.gov.au/getmedia/77f0e938-28c2-4ea6-a9e4-98a914b0c277/SCTASK2593010-Multicultural-comm-profile-report-LHD-FA.pdf

Pew Research Center. (2024). *What the data says about immigrants in the U.S.* https://www.pewresearch.org/short-reads/2024/09/27/key-findings-about-us-immigrants/

Rezaei, S. (2007). *Breaking out: The dynamics of immigrant-owned businesses.* ResearchGate. https://www.researchgate.net/profile/Shahamak-Rezaei/publication/26619167_Breaking_out_The_Dynamics_of_Immigrant_Owned_Businesses/links/5fd0bc63299bf188d4045899/Breaking-out-The-Dynamics-of-Immigrant-Owned-Businesses.pdf

Smith, A. (2016). *London borough council housing has 50-year waiting list.* World Socialist Web Site. https://www.wsws.org/en/articles/2016/12/09/hous-d09.html

Solf, B., Guerrero, L., & Sherzad, S. (2024). *Global affordable housing shortages can harm migrant reception and integration.* Migration Policy Institute.

Statistics Canada. (2021). *Census of population.* https://www12.statcan.gc.ca/census-recensement/index-eng.cfm

United Nations. (2020). *World economic situation and prospects 2020.* https://www.un.org/development/desa/dpad/publication/world-economic-situation-and-prospects-2020

Ylanan, A., & Kambhampati, S. (2024). *How Los Angeles County became home to the biggest AAPI communities in the country.*

Los Angeles Times.
https://www.latimes.com/california/story/2024-05-15/how-southern-california-became-home-to-the-biggest-aapi-communities-in-the-country

Chapter Ten

Adminm. (2024). *Exploring the staple foods of the major African regions: A culinary journey.* Uganda Grocery Online. https://ugandagroceryonline.com/exploring-the-staple-foods-of-all-54-african-countries-a-culinary-journey/?srsltid=AfmBOooYTlIMgvwJWHs0RtZ_y2hxc MAhUeVnlJvZb6Oa7geWiC6XvZ0L

Capilla Garcia, E. (2025). *Traditions and celebrations in Mexico.* Prezi. https://prezi.com/p/o1utqgolgduq/traditions-and-celebrations-in-mexico/

Chef Tris. (2024). *Unveiling the essence of French dining culture: More than just a meal.* Eat Like the French. https://eatlikethefrench.com/the-essence-of-french-dining-culture

Dima Shariff. (2011). *Mezze culture: A Mediterranean thing.* https://www.dimasharif.com/mezze-culture/

Languages Alive. (n.d.). *The Italian family: A tapestry of tradition, love, and togetherness.* https://www.languagesalive.com/the-italian-family/

Osahon, V. (2024). *Jollof rice is more than just food.* Kennesaw State University Digital Commons. https://digitalcommons.kennesaw.edu/cgi/viewcontent.cgi?article=1045&context=engl1101

Sitges Luxury Rentals. (2023). *What are Spanish tapas? Everything you need to know.* https://sitgesluxuryrentals.com/what-are-

spanish-
tapas/#:~:text=The%20origins%20of%20tapas%20can%2
0be%20traced,prevent%20his%20subjects%20from%20b
ecoming%20overly%20drunk.&text=Tapas%20are%20an
%20important%20part%20of%20Spanish,and%20spendi
ng%20time%20with%20friends%20and%20family.

Stajcic, N. (2013). *Understanding culture: Food as a means of
communication.*
https://d1wqtxts1xzle7.cloudfront.net/55412051/05-
Stajcic_v01-libre.pdf?1514731148=&response-content-
disposition=inline%3B+filename%3DUnderstanding_Cult
ure_Food_as_a_Means_of.pdf&Expires=1736479932&Sig
nature=TH0-
PvmC4lpPVDYqu8ksLIf49JRWQvbUx13s~pnBkA-
i0I4DXdt-
lxeMLTNbG0Zq4KUPLN7aWk9GVOpIHkplg3RFr8U-
OhRagmEifanCYsMzJs-wqw2MbGA3c0nr96iYOnOut-
pNHBPS93xk3CQvFFO7TNzMCdhAObGatLiYs5SFQ
Kz9~pEUCgkWjHux9FiF6PlbD6ouF-
3DJoCgPhAl23AZuLmEgTDgM-iePH8CD-
icLh4RsXvLrGQkBHAkWbrRWjDfD3rxHGhCIL-
9cygZEMpFx1LsKsNFt-Q7LL0d0w-
JO~B4aPdSalJh8nYYznGnEvNiKqGNPtgXJ2yjReuf2A
&Key-Pair-Id=APKAJLOHF5GGSLRBV4ZA

UBC. (2024). *The intersection of culture and cuisine: How food shapes
our identity.* University of British Columbia.
https://arts.ubc.ca/news/the-intersection-of-culture-and-
cuisine-how-food-shapes-our-identity/

UNESCO. (n.d.). *Food culture: 30 amazing culinary traditions around the world.* Wander-Lush. https://wander-lush.org/food-culture-unesco/

Unknown Author. (2023). *The ultimate guide to Japanese food: A culinary journey.* Japan Specialist. https://japanspecialist.com/w/the-ultimate-guide-to-japanese-food

www.ingramcontent.com/pod-product-compliance
Lightning Source LLC
Chambersburg PA
CBHW051005140626
46546CB00016B/719